Praise for Norm Trainor's
The 8 Best Practices of High-Performing Salespeople

*"On my return from Singapore to Zurich,
I found your manuscript waiting on my desk...
I do wish I had been able to read it sooner because
I would have liked to have been able to share
some of the advice with the 500 people I had trained
in Singapore and the 750 people in Bratislava. I regard
your book very highly and would recommend it to any
person who is interested in becoming a true professional
in the insurance industry. They will benefit from the
expertise and experience you have successfully
reproduced in this book."*

**Eric Westacott,
International Life Insurance Marketing Adviser,
Representing the largest life & health reinsurance company in the world**

"You are an incredible writer! You can spin a story so well that I can't wait to turn the page and see what happens next. And it all makes sense! Once I began reading the book, I could not put it down until I was finished. You speak great truths about what works for high-performing salespeople. This is not just a book of how-to's, but a clear philosophy of what makes a successful businessperson. You make your points well, and the stories you use to describe the process are compelling — something that everyone of us can identify with. It has already helped me re-focus on important issues in my own business, and it will benefit every single salesperson and businessperson who reads it."

Mary Lou Gutscher, President,
M L Communications Inc.

"This book is must-reading for anyone wanting to excel at sales. With remarkable clarity, Norm Trainor gives the clues to the inner conflicts that every so often block our success. The book provides a path with proven strategies for facilitating decision making with today's more informed and sophisticated clientele."

Dave Reid, President,
Equinox Financial Group

"The 8 Best Practices of High-Performing Salespeople *identifies the need to plan for success, earn the right to be of service, to honor your commitments, and to effectively self-manage. Norm Trainor's philosophy is right on – it's the only way to achieve high quality relationships that result in mutually beneficial results."*

June Donaldson, MBA, President,
Donaldson & Associates, Inc.

THE 8
BEST PRACTICES
OF HIGH
PERFORMING
SALESPEOPLE

Also coauthored by Donald Cowper and Andrew Haynes

_____

DAVID COWPER'S *BREAKTHROUGH*

YOUTH VIOLENCE: HOW TO PROTECT YOUR KIDS

NORM TRAINOR
with Donald Cowper and Andrew Haynes

THE 8
BEST PRACTICES
OF HIGH
PERFORMING
SALESPEOPLE

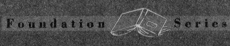

Foundation Series

HiGHRISE BOOKS™

THE 8 BEST PRACTICES OF HIGH-PERFORMING SALESPEOPLE

A HIGHRISE book

Published by DNA Creative
621 Milverton Blvd., Toronto, Ontario, M4C 1X8, Canada

TRAINOR, NORM
The 8 Best Practices of High-Performing Salespeople

ISBN 0-9682030-1-9
copyright ©1998 by DNA Creative

Design by Late Harvest Entertainment

Printed and bound in Canada

About the authors

NORM TRAINOR

Norm Trainor began his career as a sales professional in the life insurance business in 1970 and was a member of the Million Dollar Round Table. In 1975 he left the insurance business to help other salespeople become high performers. He began Wilson Learning Corporation's Canadian operation in 1975 and not only became their managing director, but was also Wilson Learning Corporation's leading salesperson. He is now a principal of The Covenant Group, specializing in sales-force effectiveness, change management and customized learning programs. He has worked with the 20 largest life insurance companies in Canada, the 5 largest banks, and a number of trust companies, mutual funds and securities dealers. In addition, he has worked extensively in the computer, telecommunications, office products and automotive industries. Norm's academic background includes post-graduate work in psychology and the behavioral sciences. He speaks at conferences and seminars around the world and writes regular columns for the *Canadian HR Reporter* and *Investment Executive*. He lives in Toronto with his wife Wendy and their three children, Ryan, Shauna and Sloan.

DONALD COWPER

Donald Cowper, a former insurance broker, is now a writer, and coauthor with David Cowper and Andrew Haynes of *Breakthrough*. He is also the coauthor with Kevin Guest and Andrew Haynes of *Youth Violence: How To Protect Your Kids*. He lives in Toronto with his girlfriend and editor, Ann Margaret.

ANDREW HAYNES

Andrew Haynes, former publisher of *The Species Review*, a Canadian high-tech magazine, is a writer, and coauthor of *Breakthrough* and *Youth Violence: How To Protect Your Kids*. He lives in Toronto with his wife, Christine.

Acknowledgments

There are a number of people to whom I am indebted in writing this book. Donald Cowper and Andrew Haynes have been wonderful partners in its creation. They have toiled long and hard.

For their special contributions, I would like to thank my wife, Wendy, and our children, Ryan, Shauna and Sloan, who have been my inspiration. As well, I would like to thank the rest of our family for their support and encouragement: my mother and father, my brother, John, my grandparents, uncle Jack, uncle Bruce and aunt Kathleen, and uncle Phil, as well as Wendy's parents and siblings.

I believe strongly in the power of mentor relationships and would like to acknowledge the debt I owe to my own mentors: David B. Cowper, S. Ross Johnson, John R. Ross, David Reid, Grant Sylvester, Dan Chabot, Larry Wilson and Bob Stock.

Although I can't mention everybody who has helped me along the way, I would like to say thank you to my colleagues and friends: Geoff Davidson, Gary Furlong, Jim Harrison, George Goldsmith, Herb Koplowitz, Karen Lee, Jack Fleming and Nick Poppenk.

Thanks to Leonid Rozenberg for the design of this book and to Ann Margaret Oberst for her expert editing. However, I take full responsibility for any errors that still remain in the book.

Donald and Andrew would like to extend their heartfelt thanks to Ann Margaret and Christine for all their encouragement, love and invaluable assistance throughout the many long days of this project.

Norm Trainor

To Wendy, who supports and challenges me to become as much as I can be.

*"Those who know
and do not act
truly do not know"*

Chinese Proverb

*"Success is something you
just had to be and
I would spend myself
unknowingly"*

John Prine

The 8 Best Practices of High-Performing Salespeople

From the earliest days of my career as an insurance agent in the early 1970s, I have always been fascinated by what makes high-performing salespeople great. For the past 22 years, as a training and development consultant, I have done extensive research into the reasons why top salespeople are successful. From that research, I have distilled the 8 best practices of high-performing salespeople. These best practices, and the strategies that I outline to put them into action, are universal, applicable to all fields and all businesses.

Throughout this book, I sometimes refer to products, concepts, and laws that may or may not apply to your particular area.

The cases I describe in this book are based on real events, however, in order to protect the privacy and confidentiality of my clients, I have changed all their names and all the telling details of the stories. I have also changed the names of everyone else in this book, except for my own and those of my wife, Wendy, my son, Ryan, and David Cowper.

Contents

He would find out
whether or not he could
sell himself to a multimillionaire
and break through to
higher income levels.

Chapter 1

The 8 Best Practices of High-Performing Salespeople

Nine years ago, I began working with a young salesman named Tony Henderson to help him become a high-performing salesperson. Back then, Tony was stuck at a middle income level and was eager to break through to six and, eventually, seven-figure earnings. I remember sitting down with Tony and discussing what behaviors he needed to change in order to reach his goals. We focused on something I had developed from my years of research into what makes a top salesperson a top salesperson. What I discovered was that the hundreds of high performers I studied all did the same things. I have come to call their behaviors the 8 Best Practices of high-performing salespeople. Tony was eager to put those practices into action, and immediately arranged a meeting with the owner of a local business worth $90,000,000. Let me tell you the story of that meeting.

The $90,000,000 challenge

Tony took a deep breath and stepped into Ivan Kapeck's empty office. It was 9:28 AM. He was two minutes early. The wall facing him was a vast expanse of glass looking out over a clear, blue lake. In the distance a speed boat skimmed across the surface, the white spray arcing behind it. The scene was beautiful but did little to settle his jangling nerves. In front of the window a wide oak desk and two leather executive chairs sat empty. He walked quickly across the thick beige carpet and took a seat.

His right hand clutched the handle of the briefcase cradled in his lap. A nervous sweat prickled the back of his neck. Although he was only 30 years old, he believed that the fate of his career in the mutual fund industry depended on this meeting. He would find out whether or not he could sell himself to a multimillionaire and break through to higher income levels. The man he was waiting for, Ivan Kapeck, was the most important prospect he had ever arranged a meeting with. An expectant chill ran up Tony's spine. When he left the office in 45 minutes he hoped to have his first multi-million-dollar client.

Up till now, Tony had been selling to people with much lower incomes. He had been concentrating on his natural market — people his own age who were making an average of $50,000 a year. He felt comfortable selling to his peers because he knew them, understood what made them tick, and how to talk to them. They were the people he'd gone to school with, played sports with, and worked with in the summers. In the past year he'd made a decent living, but their limited incomes put a limit on what Tony could earn. They only had so much money to invest in mutual funds. They were at the sunrise of their careers, had barely begun professional lives that might lead to huge success. Tony didn't want to lose them as clients, but, with a new wife and a baby on the way, he was eager to increase his income. Plus, he wanted to learn and grow as a financial planner. For that, he would need to work on more complex and challenging cases. He was now angling for bigger fish. That's what brought him here, into foreign territory, to visit Ivan Kapeck. The thought excited him, but made him ill at the same time.

As Tony waited for Mr. Kapeck to arrive, he rubbed his sweaty palms against the woolen pants of his suit. He had been researching Kapeck and preparing for this meeting for weeks. He felt that he now had the tools to sell Mr. Kapeck, but he knew that it would be impossible, unless he managed to do one thing — earn Mr. Kapeck's respect. And in order to do that, he had to overcome one major problem.

The problem was that Mr. Kapeck had known Tony for 25 years, but as his son's friend. Tony realized it would be difficult to get Mr. Kapeck to see him as a trusted financial advisor, instead of one of his son's wild friends who used to stay out past curfew, sneak wine from the basement cellar and who was always horsing around in their backyard pool. Tony knew that, although his acquaintance with John had enabled him to get this meeting, he had to distance himself from those days and change Mr. Kapeck's view of him.

Suddenly Mr. Kapeck burst into the room. A scowl knitted his brow. Behind him, his secretary hurried to close the doors. A small bubble caught in Tony's throat as Mr. Kapeck strode quickly towards him. Mr. Kapeck was even bigger than Tony remembered — 6'2", 220 pounds, gray hair, and a thick neck heaving over a starched white shirt collar and the tight knot of his bright red tie. Under his bushy, dark eyebrows his green eyes bulged. Tony was possessed by a sudden, irrational fear.

As Mr. Kapeck reached the desk, Tony stood stiffly to greet him. He reached out a moist hand and tried to smile.

"Hello, kid," Mr. Kapeck said gruffly and then released Tony's hand, brushed past him and took a seat on the other side of his desk.

Tony winced at the 'kid' reference. He knew things wouldn't be easy. "Hello, Mr. Kapeck," he began, but was cut off.

"I don't have a lot of time, Henderson," Kapeck said, slipping on his glasses and looking down at a file in front of him. "You want to talk about my finances, that right?"

"Well, yes, I. . . . Yes actually, I did. But. . ." Tony paused. He really needed Kapeck to start treating him like he was somebody who could help, rather than some kid wasting his time. "Mr. Kapeck," Tony began, "I'm here to offer you my services as a financial planner."

Mr. Kapeck sighed and pulled off his glasses, one arm at a time. "Why would I need your help? I already have lots of experienced people looking after my money."

Tony's stomach collapsed in on itself. He squirmed in his chair.

"You're my kid's friend and that's why I let you come and see me." Tony nodded slightly. He knew enough to let Mr. Kapeck speak while he listened for an opportunity. "But I don't need another college-educated, money man taking a slice of my business."

Tony's spirits brightened. This was his opening. He would have to strike now, and accurately. "I'm not here to take another slice out of your business, Mr. Kapeck. I'm here to help you build an empire outside your business — your personal estate." Tony saw Mr. Kapeck nod briefly with interest. "You see, you have done an incredible thing. You've built a wildly successful business on your own. You started this company when you were only 17, hauling junk and then freight around Muskoka. After you had built it up from one old pickup to a fleet of 18-wheel rigs shipping across the country, you began to branch out. You diversified into car dealerships and restaurants. And now, I'd estimate you're worth close to $90,000,000."

Across the desk Mr. Kapeck smiled in spite of himself. "I can see you've done some homework," he said. This was the first good sign. Tony felt himself gaining momentum. Here's where he could get Mr. Kapeck to see him as a professional.

"Mr. Kapeck, you are the reason your business has grown. It was your years and years of hard work that took your company to the $90,000,000 level. The problem is, the company still needs you to continue growing. It is your constant effort that keeps your business profitable. You probably spend most of your time at the office and when you're not here you're still thinking about your company, worrying about what could go wrong, and trying to guess what disaster might strike next so you can head it off before it destroys your business."

Mr. Kapeck nodded again.

"If you are like most successful business owners," Tony said, "you're probably so busy with your business that you don't have time to pay attention to your personal finances."

Mr. Kapeck said, "I suppose you're right, but I make 30% on every dollar I put back into my business. Why would I put my dollars anywhere else?"

Tony knew this was where he could swing things in his favor. He had prepared himself for this type of objection. "Mr. Kapeck," he began, "let me explain it this way. I'm sure you are familiar with the Gibson fiasco. Like you, he put everything back into his business because it was growing so quickly. It looked like it was never going to end. But the market slipped, and suddenly Mr. Gibson was in trouble. Banks started calling loans, his suppliers stopped giving him credit, and he had to sell all his assets. In the end, he was left with nothing."

Tony saw Mr. Kapeck lean forward — now he was listening. Tony kept going. "Gibson's problem was he never offset the risk in his business. He did not build up an estate outside his business. Mr. Kapeck, you have dealt well with risk inside your business. You have diversified and built up several streams of revenue, so that a loss in one area does not wipe you out. However, no business is bulletproof, and were your businesses ever to suffer, you would suffer some personal financial trouble. What we can do is work together to extend the management of your risk outside your business. Just like you are diversifying inside your business, we can diversify outside your business. We can reduce your risk by building up your personal assets, so that your fate does not rely solely on your business. This will give you peace of mind. Plus, it will give you the freedom to leave the business when you choose — with your financial affairs in order."

Mr. Kapeck rubbed his chin thoughtfully.

"Unfortunately, Mr. Kapeck, I don't think the business can afford to give you some time off to take care of your finances. On top of that, your expertise lies in managing your business, and that's exactly what you should be doing. What I'm suggesting is you let someone who is capable do with your personal finances what you're doing right now with your business. . . . And that person is me. That's the reason I'm here today — I want to be your personal financial advisor."

"I already have advisors — an accountant, a stockbroker, an insurance agent," Kapeck said.

"I'm sure your advisors are doing a good job in their area of expertise, but what you need is someone to look at your entire financial situation. You need someone who can make sure all the pieces of your financial puzzle are working together. You need someone who can look at your will to make sure it is going to achieve what you want, and someone who can help put together things like an estate freeze to minimize taxes and protect your heirs. These are all the things I will be able to do for you." Tony finished, and sat back in his chair.

There was silence. Tony waited. He didn't twitch, didn't move. There were only a few more minutes left in their meeting. The ball was in Mr. Kapeck's court now. Tony waited patiently.

Suddenly Mr. Kapeck broke into a smile. "You know, Tony, no

one's ever spoken to me like that before about my money. Certainly not a 30-year-old kid. I didn't know John had friends as smart as you." Mr. Kapeck rose from his chair and walked over to the far window, his back turned to Tony.

Tony closed his eyes, and braced himself.

"Tony," Mr. Kapeck said, still gazing out the window, "why don't you go and put a plan together for my personal finances. If I like what I see, you've got the job."

"Mr. Kapeck, before we put together a plan for you, I need to better understand your situation. Would it be all right if I asked you a few questions? It will take about an hour or two. Do you have time now, or should we reschedule for another day?"

Mr. Kapeck continued to stare out the window, then turned around. "Let's take the time now, Tony. Fire away!"

"Thank you, Mr. Kapeck," Tony said.

"Tony, call me Ivan."

Tony left the meeting, knowing he had accomplished one of his goals for that day — Mr. Kapeck no longer considered him merely as his son's friend. He had gained his trust. His second goal — getting the business — would depend on his plan. He knew he could do that. A few weeks later, he was working as Mr. Kapeck's financial advisor. Tony was thrilled. He had only just begun using the 8 Best Practices of high-performing salespeople and already he was on his way to success.

The 8 Best Practices

After closing the Kapeck deal, Tony continued to close large deals with other older, very wealthy clients. Over the years he realized his dream of a seven-figure income. Today, Tony is 39 and owns a financial planning company that employs 25 young mutual fund and insurance salespeople and controls over $300 million in assets — $115 million of which is under Tony's personal management. Tony attributes his current success to the fact that he changed his behavior and put the 8 Best Practices of high-performing salespeople into action. In fact, I now consider Tony to be an exemplar of the 8 Best Practices. Tony is proof that by simply adopting the behavior of successful people you too can become successful. Throughout this book, we'll be exploring in depth exactly what those practices are. We'll take a look at how Tony used them to close the Kapeck deal and others. We'll also see how many of my other clients have utilized the 8 Best Practices to break through to new levels of success. But before we can do this, there is something crucial we have to look at.

When I uncovered
my inner conflict, I was able to
begin changing the direction of my life. . . .
Awareness is power, and I am continually
seeking deeper self-awareness, so that I can
gain greater and greater control
over my life, my destiny.

Chapter 2

What you want is what you get

E ven before you can begin putting the 8 Best Practices of high-performing salespeople to work for you, you must do something very crucial — you must be clear that you *want* to become a high-performing salesperson. You must have what I call a clear intention to succeed. People who lack clarity about their intention find themselves stalling out. In my 22 years of training salespeople, I have learned that as many as 9 out of 10 of them feel they can do so much better than they are. Many of them think they are not succeeding because of external circumstances, such as a struggling economy, unemployment, saturated markets, or too much competition. However, most of the time, their problem lies inside them, not outside. The real reason they are not successful is because they are not clear about what they want.

As a trainer, I meet many salespeople who think they know what they want, but who, in fact, lack clarity. I can tell they aren't clear about their desire to succeed because they are not doing the things necessary for success. People who have clarity are always moving toward the success they are seeking.

There are various reasons why someone might lack a clear intention. Sometimes it is because they don't have a plan, or are not following a plan, or simply don't know what they should be doing. Other times their lack of clarity stems from an inner conflict. Even though someone might think they want to be successful, there may be something in their subconscious that is getting in the way. They may harbor a fear of failure, or even a fear of success. Inner conflict can be a serious roadblock to success. In order to realize your potential, you must resolve any inner conflicts you might have. You must be able to focus all your energies on achieving your goals of success.

In the next chapter we'll explore how you can clarify your intentions through planning. In this chapter we'll take a look at how inner conflicts can work against your desire for success. Let me begin by telling you my story. I am someone who knows firsthand the damage inner conflict can cause.

Let's go back to one Sunday in the early '80s — a rather monumental day in my life.

The avalanche that nearly brought the house down

Rain pelted the window behind me. It was a Sunday afternoon late in the summer, and I sat slumped in the sofa in our front living room. Even though it was only shortly past noon, the dark rain clouds made it feel like late evening. There was a dull throb at the back of my head; it had come on a few days ago and never left. With my tired, aching eyes, I surveyed the living room, with its newly varnished wood flooring, the freshly painted walls, the wainscoting, the cornices. It was exactly what we had wanted — it was a dream, but the dream had become a nightmare.

Overhead, I heard the pattering of my son's feet scurrying to the staircase, then his footfalls as he thumped excitedly down each step. He came into view, leaping from the last step onto the main floor. He was wearing only his socks and he slid a few feet in my direction. He was beaming a great big smile. He was six years old, happy it was Sunday, and happier that his dad was home. We hadn't seen each other much in the past few months.

"Daddy," said Ryan, "play with me."

I took a long look at him, his excited expression glowing with innocence — an innocence that was in such stark contrast to the way I was now feeling that my heart began to ache deeply. Here we were in this gorgeous house that we had just renovated. It should have been a happy moment — a father and his son in their new home on a Sunday afternoon. But I knew something that Ryan didn't know. I knew that this house might not be ours for much longer. My thoughts turned to the renovations — the months of constant renovations. The renovations that were supposed to cost only $70,000, but ended up costing three times that — taking my wife and me to the brink of financial ruin.

When we purchased the original house — a triplex — it was in poor condition. We knew it needed a complete overhaul. It was an ambitious project, but at the time we felt we could do anything we set our minds to. I'd had a string of great years, and saw no reason to think my income wouldn't keep skyrocketing. We gutted the house, stripped it bare, leaving only the outside walls standing. I remembered seeing it then, thinking that it looked like a movie-set prop house. I looked forward to watching it all come together. Then, layer by layer, floorboard by floorboard, we rebuilt it. Unfortunately, during the whole process, it wasn't my income that rose, but the cost of the renovations. My income was going the other way — down. And it was going down fast, for reasons I'll explain later. We had to borrow the money to finance the home and, at the time, the loan rates were a murderous 24%. And to top things off, the housing market took a dive, and the value of the home slid below the combined value of the original purchase price plus the cost of the renovations. The money pit had no bottom. And there was yet another reason for worry: I was in the process of breaking ties with my current employer, Wilson Learning, so I could strike out on my own. My future income was uncertain. Now, our renovated home, the elegance of the craftsmanship, the impressive design — all of it seemed like a grotesque mockery of the torment I felt inside. After months of struggling to keep things afloat I was exhausted, jaded. The final collapse was imminent.

The terrifying cycle in my life

"Daddy," Ryan cried. "What's wrong, Daddy?" There was panic in his voice.

"What is it, Ryan?" I asked, shaking my head as my eyes adjusted to bring him into focus.

"Daddy," he said, "you weren't moving. You were just sitting there — you were scaring me."

At first, I didn't understand what he meant, then I realized that he had probably been standing there for a couple of minutes talking to me, while I zoned out, drowning in the stress of my life. No wonder he was scared. My behavior had certainly changed over the past few months. I was not the father I used to be, always up for fun and games. Always excited to be home. Ryan's father, his hero, the man he worshipped, was crumbling under the pressure. I attempted a smile.

"Daddy's okay," I said. "Don't worry. Nothing's wrong." I assured him. But his face was still full of fear and panic — he knew that things were not all right.

"Tiger," I said, and then paused. Something was very odd about this moment. The most powerful *déjà vu* experience I'd ever had swept through me. I had lived this moment before. I was sure of it. But when? Where? And then it hit, like a wave crashing over me. I had lived it indeed. But it was nearly 30 years ago. And it wasn't Ryan standing there. It was me, as a 6-year-old boy. And the man on the couch was my grandfather.

I reached down and grabbed Ryan, and held him tight against my chest. A maelstrom of emotions erupted inside of me. All the negative feelings that had dominated my life in the past few months — the fear, the anger, the self-loathing — were now mixed with a great sense of relief and release. At last I realized what was happening to my life. Some part of me must have known what was going on all along, but I just hadn't seen it. And now it was as clear as ever — the financial trouble we were in was my subconscious attempt to recreate my past. As I sat here with Ryan, I sensed that my life had come full circle.

I could picture so clearly the image of my grandfather on the couch — slumped in the cushions, his eyes empty, staring. "Granda," I remember calling over and over again, but there was no answer. He was lost, my own hero, always full of such strength, was now crumpled — weary and beaten. Something had happened to him — I had no idea what, but I knew it wasn't good. And I was right. Dark, ugly days followed that moment. My childhood as I had known it ended that day.

The dark, ugly days of my childhood

As Ryan clung to me on the sofa, and the rain fell hard outside, my childhood came flooding back to me. When I was a little boy — before everything turned black — I lived with my parents in a small home in a small town in Northern Ireland, on a street built by my grandfather, who was in the construction business. He lived on the same street, but on the corner lot. I spent a lot of my childhood in his house, which I loved because it was big and always full of sunlight which streamed in through the large windows. It was so different from my parents' home which was cramped and dark, and filled with the strained emotions of my parents' unhappy marriage. I felt safe and happy with my grandfather; we loved each other a lot, and were very close.

I remembered summer days on his porch, eating the biscuits my grandmother made and drinking tea with lots of milk and sugar, and listening to Granda's stories, of the days before cars and airplanes and television. He always wore a cap proudly on his head, and I would beg him to let me wear it for a few minutes. I would fill with pride when he handed it to me, the brim flopping over my eyes so I couldn't see. I would hear him laugh, a deep laugh, as I marched up and down the porch smothered in his cap, pretending to be him. Some days my brother, our friends and I would play in Granda's side lot. We'd play war, using wooden guns, and a rusty old wheelbarrow as a tank.

But the day I saw my grandfather on the couch was the last day of fun. That night, I was shuttled off to live with my great-grandparents in a tiny village a few miles away. I didn't really know what was happening, but I knew my grandfather was gone. He went to live in another country, Canada. And so did my father and mother. I would not see my parents or my grandfather for many months. I didn't see many of my friends ever again. I was sick with loneliness, and spent many nights crying myself to sleep.

Years later I would learn what had happened. My grandfather had lost everything. In 1952, when I was 6, a recession had hit Great Britain, but my grandfather continued to grow his business, borrowing money and building homes at an accelerated rate. He was grossly overextended, and when people stopped buying his homes, his suppliers demanded immediate payment. He was a proud man, and wanted to make good on all his commitments, so he liquidated everything, and paid off all his creditors. As a businessman he was finished in Ireland. There was no opportunity left for him there, so he emigrated to Canada.

But the death of my grandfather's business did more than destroy him financially. It killed his spirit. He was never the same again. When I finally arrived in Canada to live with my parents and see my grandfather again, I saw a different man, a broken man. He loved working for himself and building his own business, but he never managed to start a business in Canada. Instead, he struggled through various jobs, always working for someone else, which was a major source of unhappiness for him. He lived the rest of his life frustrated and depressed until he passed away at the age of 86.

The similarity of my grandfather's fate to my current position was uncanny. I had done exactly what he had done. I had risked everything, overextended myself, and now my life was about to unravel just like his. I was 6 at the time of my grandfather's ruin, and Ryan was the same age. And what disturbed me even further was what lay at the center of our financial disaster: our home — a replica of my grandfather's house. Our house, like his, was the large corner house. The exposure was the same — southeast. The entire feel of the house, its spaciousness and brightness, was the same. I was trying to recreate my grandfather's collapse — house and all.

As I sat holding Ryan, feeling the slow rhythm of his breathing against my chest, I realized what I was so afraid of. It wasn't the material loss. I could live without this house. Rather, I was terrified of ending up like my grandfather — beaten, depressed. And I was even more terrified of putting Ryan through what I had suffered as a child. I didn't want him to endure the loneliness and to watch, as I had, his role models fail and wither away.

I turned to look down at Ryan. "Really, Tiger," I said, "everything will be okay." I said it and meant it. I was determined not to follow in my grandfather's footsteps.

Ryan gave me a big squeeze, then jumped onto the floor. Sensing that I was feeling better, he was ready to play again.

Deeper into myself: success means death

After playing with Ryan, I went upstairs to my study. I wanted to be alone — I had some thinking to do. I closed the door and sat down on the small two-seater sofa, and placed my legs on the ottoman. Outside, the rain had slowed to a peaceful, lulling drizzle. Through the window I could see the top of the old maple tree swaying gently. In the quiet of the study, I reflected on my revelation earlier in the afternoon. Realizing that I had subconsciously recreated my grandfather's life was certainly a helpful first step towards identifying my inner conflict. I now knew *what* I had done, but I still had no idea *why* I had done it.

I knew the *why* of it lay deeper inside of me. Even though I thought I wanted to be personally successful, and even though it was my business as a trainer to help others succeed, I knew that somehow I possessed a subconscious desire to sabotage my own success. All my behavior pointed in that direction; otherwise I would not have behaved the way I did — recklessly overextending myself, dumping more and more money into the home, going deeper in debt. And while I was doing all of this, I was breaking away from my steady income at Wilson Learning and trying to start my own business. Why did I burden myself with all these pressures at once? Because I really didn't want to be successful. Somehow I was afraid of success. Deep down, I believed success was a bad thing. I asked myself why I believed this. The answer began to dawn on me. It had something to do with what I had learned as a child from my father.

As I sat in the study, meditating about my father, childhood memories began to surface. One Thursday evening during my high-school years came back clearly.

Success is a bad thing

I ran ahead, down the sidewalk, to grab my football before it bounced onto the street. I was carrying my muddy football gear. The field had been wet and mucky, and it had been a pretty crazy game — more like mud wrestling than football. In the end, our team had won. I couldn't wait to get home to tell my father.

When I stepped through the doorway, I shouted, "We won!"

My mom was in the kitchen making dinner and couldn't hear me, but my dad was in the living room reading. He shouted back, "Great, son."

"We destroyed them," I yelled.

"What was the score?" he asked excitedly.

"28 to 3," I said, as I walked in and sat down in the chair next to him. "That's amazing. . . . How many tackles did you make?"

"Four."

My father loved to talk about football. He had been an athlete when he was younger. He was the light-heavyweight boxing champion of Ireland, and would have turned pro and gone to the Olympic Games, but the Olympics were called off that year because of WWII. I worked hard at sports so he could be proud of me — and he was. He was always encouraging me to excel.

After our discussion of the game, my father returned to the newspaper. I turned on the TV. After a few minutes, my father shook his head disapprovingly. "Look at this, son," he said glancing down at one of the newspaper articles, "this guy here, Mr. Owens, bought a printing company that was in trouble last month, said he was going to turn things around. Well, he turned things upside down, that's for sure — he just closed the business down — fired everybody, and sold all the equipment. He just made a quick fortune, and all these people are out of work now. What a son-of-a-bitch." He continued shaking his head.

A few moments later, Dad started grunting. "J. Portland, you know that rich guy, merchant banker. . . . " I didn't know who he was talking about, but I was sure my father had mentioned him before. ". . . . died yesterday. Only 47. Died of a heart attack. You see what all that money does." He glanced up at me, I nodded, and then my father returned to the newspaper.

After a while, he put the paper down on the coffee table, leaned back in his chair, and glared up at the ceiling. "You know, son, you've really got to be a son-of-a-bitch to get ahead. I'm not as successful as I could have been, but I'm no son-of-a-bitch." The words hung in the air. A few quiet minutes passed, then my father closed his eyes for a nap. I got up, padded carefully across the floor, and went to my room to read until dinner.

As I sat in the study, thinking about the things my father told me, I realized that they had a great impact on me. The stories he told me about successful people led me to believe that success would turn you into a son-of-a-bitch, or that it would cause heart failure. I grew up believing that success ruins you.

It was strange that my father would give me conflicting messages. On the one hand, he would always encourage me to be successful, not only in sports, but in all the things I did. On the other hand, he would also show me through his stories that success was a bad thing. I wondered why my father would tell me two different things. As I thought about this question, I realized that he was doing it to protect me. In his own life, he felt he never realized his true potential. He had tried various things, struggled, and eventually resigned himself to never achieving his goals. In some way, he thought he was a failure, and he didn't want me to feel the same way. By warning me that success ruins you, he was sending me the message that I should avoid it, that it wasn't worth it. In part, it was a way for him to justify why he wasn't successful.

I finally understood why I had sabotaged my success. I did it because I was afraid that it would turn me into a son-of-a-bitch or destroy my health. Part of me wanted and sought the success I had achieved, but another part of me was afraid of it.

I rose from the sofa in the study, walked toward the window, and looked down. I stood there, silently, staring at the puddles of rain on the street below. In my mind, I formed a picture of myself — of two warring halves: one striving for success, the other trying desperately to avoid it. This was me, and this explained why I had been sabotaging my life. Before I purchased the house, my income had been rising. A few years earlier, I had opened up the Canadian operation of Wilson Learning. Over the following few years I had personally grown the operation from nothing into a multi-million-dollar business. I was a success, and becoming more of one. What I didn't know was that the more successful I became, the more my hidden desire to avoid success kicked in. I had to do something about it, and I did. I went about undoing my success, the best way I knew how — the way my grandfather had done it.

The difference between failing and failure

The more I thought about my father, the more I realized that he had made a big mistake in thinking of himself as a failure. He may have failed, but failing doesn't make you a failure. It is certainly true that my father experienced hardship and loss, but his error was in taking it all personally. He identified himself with his hardships and believed he was getting what he deserved. If he had looked at the situation differently, he would have realized that as a person he was worth something — no matter what his circumstances were. Had he taken this approach, he would have been able to endure the hardships, and look for new opportunities. He should have realized that it is okay to fail, that he was not a failure because he failed.

As I gazed out into the rain, I understood that failing is a part of life, that we all fail at things, and that failing should never stop us from trying to succeed. When you try to succeed, you may fail, but you are not a failure. If you realize that, you will be able to try again. Eventually you will succeed, but you may have failed many times along the way.

When I came down from that study after meditating on my past, I possessed something vital that I hadn't had that morning — self-awareness. I was aware now of my subconscious desire to avoid success, and how this desire had directed my behavior and put my happiness and my family's happiness in jeopardy. I also knew that I had nothing to fear from failing. If I failed, it did not mean I was a failure. It would not be a catastrophic event, it would not change me as a person. I would be able to deal with it, and move on.

I had begun the process of figuring out what I really wanted in my life, a process that would change my life forever — and for the better.

Self-awareness is power

The day I spent on the couch with Ryan and later in the study by myself took place over fifteen years ago; and I was right — my life did change. Today, we still have the house, and I am running a thriving business.

Things changed because I had gained self-awareness. With this new awareness, I was able to figure out what I wanted — what I truly wanted, not what I was taught to want — out of life. I realized that I wanted to be truly successful. And for me, as for most of us, success does not mean simply material wealth. It means a happy family, physical, mental, and spiritual health, and the freedom to do what we want with our lives. At that time, 15 years ago, I knew my first steps towards my goal of success involved saving our house and getting our financial state in order. I put an immediate stop to my reckless risk taking, and began to focus my energies on growing my business, and earning the money to pay off all our debts. I was clear about what I wanted, and I made sure everything I did helped me achieve my goal. Armed with self-awareness and a greater understanding of why I behaved in certain ways, I was able to stop myself before acting in ways that would have sabotaged my success. I was running in one direction only — toward success. My intention was clear.

Why knowing what you want is so important

I have often asked myself what would have happened to me and my family had I not had my revelation that Sunday afternoon 15 years ago. I honestly believe that I would never have allowed myself to keep the house and run a successful, lucrative business on my own. At best, I would have found some sort of compromise, a state of half-success, where my two opposing desires met at an equilibrium — where I believed I was successful enough to live decently and earn my father's respect, and at the same, where my success was not great enough to make me believe I was becoming a son-of-a-bitch or developing a heart condition. At worst, I would have completed my re-enactment of my grandfather's fate, lost the house, lost my business, disrupted my family, and settled into a life of depression and failure. Fortunately, neither of these two fates occurred.

When I uncovered my inner conflict, I was able to begin changing the direction of my life. But the process of resolving inner conflict is an ongoing one — you don't just suddenly figure yourself out one day and live happily ever after. The fear of success I learned as a child is still a part of me. It is something I continue to deal with. Since that Sunday 15 years ago, I have spent many other afternoons with myself, discovering and rediscovering who I am, what I want. Awareness is power, and I am continually seeking deeper self-awareness, so that I can gain greater and greater control over my life, my destiny.

The sales profession: success and failure on a daily basis

Over the course of my career as a trainer, I have related the story of my struggle with success to other sales professionals, many of whom were able to see a bit of themselves in my story. Although they didn't have the same upbringing as I had, they saw parallels and similarities. They, too, had unresolved issues — often specifically concerning success — that were limiting their ability to achieve their goals. For a long while, I was amazed at the number of people in the sales industry who could identify with my story. I am not so amazed any more; I have come to realize that the sales profession tends to attract people who are in some way emotionally wounded. I think this happens because sales is a profession where you are forced to confront success and failure on a daily basis.

Many people enter the sales profession, not simply as a way to earn a living, but as a way of dealing with their desire for, and fear of, success. In sales, every single day is a new opportunity for both success and failure; while the rewards can be great, the failures can be devastating. In sales, you control the level of your success, you are one hundred percent responsible. If you subconsciously feel you are becoming too successful, you will make an adjustment — you will stop closing cases. If you feel that you aren't successful enough — you will work harder and smarter and make the sales you need. This type of behavior leads to a very stressful career. Instead of always doing the things necessary to make yourself successful, you are constantly reacting to your circumstances. To avoid getting caught up in an emotional roller coaster, salespeople must realize their true self-worth and understand that they are not defined by their outward success or failure.

I have always found it ironic that many salespeople end up doing things that mess up their financial affairs, especially since it is their job to sort out other people's finances. My behavior during the '80s is a good example of this irony. As a sales trainer and former financial planner, I should have known better than to overextend myself. But, like many others, I found it difficult to take my own advice — not because the advice wasn't sound, but because it went against my subconscious desire to avoid success.

A few years ago, I came across a salesperson who had a tendency for fouling up. I'd like to turn to him now — his name is Alvin.

Alvin: a disaster waiting to happen

I met Alvin a few years ago after conducting a seminar with a group of life insurance sales professionals. He said he was experiencing some trouble in his business and asked me for some one-on-one consultation. Alvin turned out to be a classic case of inner conflict. He was a driven man, outwardly determined to be successful, yet he was doing things that jeopardized the success of his business. There was no reason his business should not have been thriving. No reason, that is, other than him.

Alvin worked in a small brokerage office. There were probably half-a-dozen other agents there, and a support staff of five. Alvin was in his middle 30s and had been in the insurance business for five years. Although his first couple of years were a struggle, they were followed by two very strong years. Unfortunately, things were now heading downhill. He was having trouble closing cases, and couldn't figure out why. To him, it was a mystery — to me, the answer quickly became obvious. In fact, he gave me some tell-tale clues on the day of our first appointment.

Alvin and I arranged to meet for our preliminary session on a Thursday afternoon at 3:00. At 2:55, I stepped through the front doors of the agency office and approached the receptionist's desk.

"Hi, I'm Norm Trainor. I'm here to see Alvin. We have a three o'clock meeting," I said.

I noticed that the receptionist rolled her eyes slightly at the mention of Alvin's name. Alvin and the receptionist were obviously not best of friends. Not a good sign, I thought to myself.

"Take a seat, Mr. Trainor, Alvin will be a *while*." She put a strong emphasis on the word 'while.'

I sat down in one of the lobby chairs, and reached for a copy of today's paper on a side table. The receptionist buzzed Alvin in his office.

"Your three o'clock is here. . . . A Mr. Trainor. . . . He's here in the lobby, right now," I heard her say, almost sarcastically. Boy, they really didn't get along. I shook my head, then proceeded to read the paper.

I read a few articles, then glanced down at my watch. It was a few minutes past three.

"Excuse me," I said, trying to get the receptionist's attention.

"He knows you're here, Mr. Trainor. I'll try him again, for what good that'll do."

She buzzed him, and I returned to my paper.

At a quarter after three, Alvin marched hurriedly into the lobby.

"Sorry," he said, sounding harried.

"Busy?" I asked as we walked past the receptionist's desk and down the hall.

"Yeah, yeah. Things are a little crazy. I'm a little behind," he replied, with frustration in his voice. "That's why I need you — to help me get ahead."

We walked into his office and sat down at his work table by the window.

"Do you find that you're late a lot, Alvin?" I asked, trying not to sound accusatory.

"I've just got so much to do. You know, the pressure is pretty heavy these days. A few months ago I was at the top of the sales ladder. There's a lot of pressure to keep that up. Once you hit that level, people expect you to keep going."

He didn't answer my question directly, but he didn't have to. I wasn't the only one he'd been late for. He was probably late for all his appointments — prospects and clients included. But he raised an interesting issue — expectations. He mentioned other people's expectations, but I wondered about his own.

"Alvin," I asked, "what did *you* expect? Did you expect to just keep improving your sales. Or did you expect you'd slip into a slump?"

"Hmmm," he replied, as he considered my question. Obviously, he hadn't given much thought to his own expectations. "Up, I guess. I'm always trying to improve my sales performance, that's for sure. I know I'm ambitious — sometimes too ambitious, I guess."

"What do you mean by that," I asked. "Too ambitious?"

"Well, I can get pretty aggressive about my business."

"Aggression and ambition are different," I said. "You can be ambitious without being aggressive."

He shook his head, disagreeing with me. "People say that, but I don't think so. I think you've got to go out and get what you want. I'm not a jerk, but if someone is wasting my time, I don't really have any patience for that. I've got a lot of business to close — and I'd better do it soon."

What about wasting *my* time, I thought. But I wasn't ready to challenge him, so I let the obvious double standard lie for the moment. To me, Alvin didn't seem like the kind of man who didn't care about other people. He wasn't that type at all. In fact, I got the impression that he was very sensitive. My feeling was that Alvin was confused — he was behaving in ways that he himself wouldn't approve of. Something was bothering him, causing him to behave in a way that didn't reflect his true personality. I wondered what was at the root of it. If we could find the answer to that riddle, we'd have the solution to his sales slump.

"Why do you have to close so much business so soon?" I asked.

"'Cause I want to get ahead," he replied.

"And what is stopping you?"

"I don't know, Norm. That's why you're here."

"Okay, Alvin, why don't we talk about a recent case you had, one you lost."

"I've lost a few big ones recently."

"Just start with one."

Blowing a big case

Alvin leaned back in his chair, and stared pensively at the ceiling. "I guess the Doherty case is as good as any," he said, shaking his head with disappointment. "You know, a few months ago, I would have been able to close it, I'm sure of it. It's weird, you know. I feel a little bit like I've lost my touch."

"Tell me about the Doherty case," I said.

"Jim Doherty is a wealthy business owner. A client of mine referred me to him. He owns a few car dealerships across the country. Flies all over the place. He's in his late 40s, has a wife, three kids and no insurance. He was a cinch, or so I thought. I had a pretty strong referral. My client, Oscar, the guy who referred me to Jim, is one of Jim's closest friends. He pretty much told Jim to buy from me. In fact, I thought I would be picking up a signed application and a check on my first appointment. But it certainly didn't turn out that way."

"What happened?" I asked. "Tell me about your first appointment."

"It was a few weeks ago. I was supposed to go down to Jim's office for a one o'clock." I didn't like the sound of the words 'supposed to.' "But I got caught in some nasty traffic."

"Where's Jim's office?"

"Out by the airport."

"Did you leave from here?" I asked.

"Yeah, why?"

"Do you remember what time you left for the appointment?"

"About 12:35, I think."

I calculated the drive to Jim's office from Alvin's office. I guessed it was a half-hour drive in no traffic.

"Why did you leave so late?"

"I was busy," he replied, frustration creeping into his voice. The Doherty case was an unpleasant memory for Alvin. "It was an unbelievable day," he continued. "I had two morning appointments and about fifteen calls to make when I got back to the office at noon. I just couldn't leave on time."

"Were all those calls you had to make urgent?" I asked.

"Yeah, sure, everything's urgent. I gotta make my calls if I'm going to sell anything."

What about closing the cases you already have, I thought again to myself. Clearly, Alvin was not focusing his energies in the right direction.

"So what happened to your Doherty appointment?"

"I got there at 1:20."

"What was Doherty's reaction?"

"Seemed a little annoyed, but I don't think it made a big difference."

"Why?"

"I don't know. I just don't think it would have changed things if I'd been on time." Alvin couldn't have been more wrong, but I didn't want to correct him at this point. I wanted to know the whole story.

"So what happened?"

"We talked about his business. I wanted to try to figure out how much insurance he needed."

"How long did your appointment go?"

"One-thirty," he replied. "It was only supposed to be a half-hour meeting, and Jim had something else at 1:30."

"So how did the appointment end?"

"I said I'd put some numbers together, and send him a quote by the end of the week."

"And did you send the quote?"

"Yes," Alvin replied timidly. He knew what my next question was going to be.

"By the end of the week?"

"I got swamped. I couldn't send it out until the week after."

"Are you surprised that Jim didn't do business with you?"

"Yes, I am," Alvin replied staunchly. "He's a good friend of one of my long-time clients. I came highly recommended."

"Yes, but you didn't make a good impression."

"No, I don't think that's it. I think Jim is the kind of guy who's not going to buy insurance period. He doesn't have any now, and he probably won't have any when he dies."

"Alvin, you have the wrong attitude," I said. "Firstly, you shouldn't go around thinking your prospects won't buy insurance, and secondly, you shouldn't underestimate the value of making a good impression."

Alvin slumped a little lower in his chair, reflecting on what I had just said. He wasn't questioning me; he knew that what I was saying was true. He was experienced enough in sales to know that impressions count, and that a positive attitude toward your prospect is crucial. He was thinking about why he was behaving the way he was.

Our time was up. I left Alvin in his office contemplating his behavior. It was good to see Alvin take the time to think about his situation. He probably hadn't taken such a moment in months. It would do him good. He was taking the first step towards identifying his inner conflict.

When I met Alvin for the second time, we began our discussion by talking about what he wanted out of life.

"I want to be successful. That's for sure," Alvin said. "In my family, there's no room for unsuccessful people. My older brother's a doctor — makes a fortune. My sister's a lawyer. My younger brother's another story. He works at a grocery, at the counter. Minimum wage. I guess it was a good job while he was in high school, but that was 10 years ago. Now it's his career. He doesn't really get along with the rest of us, mostly not with our dad. You see, my dad is a real taskmaster. He owns a small, but super-successful trading company, and works all the time. He expects nothing less from his kids. Growing up was tough. If he caught you fooling around and not doing your homework, you got grounded pretty good."

For the rest of the meeting we talked about what Alvin's childhood was like. It was clear that Alvin had a strained relationship with his father. He was eager to earn respect and love from his father, but found him impossible to please. Nothing was good enough. Alvin had promised himself that he would never turn out to be like his dad.

Alvin grew up with mixed feelings toward his dad. On the one hand, he yearned for the success that would ultimately please his father; on the other hand, he wanted to avoid becoming the cruel person he considered his dad to be. This unresolved issue was clearly at the bottom of Alvin's current dilemma. His drive for success had placed him at the top of the sales ladder, but as soon as he got there, his desire to avoid becoming his father got the better of him. Growing up and watching his father, Alvin had learned to associate success with cruelty. The solution he found to his problems was the same one I had found 15 years ago — he sabotaged his success. Ironically, in order to undo his success, Alvin, to some extent, became the person he never wanted to be. He showed disrespect to people by being late, and by not following through on his promises. And by the reactions of the receptionist, I gathered that the people around the office were beginning to dislike him.

One afternoon spent exploring your childhood is certainly not enough to heal psychic wounds. It is not my job to counsel people about their psychological problems, and Alvin wisely began seeing a professional psychologist. Rather, my role is to help people do the things that will help them achieve their goals. But before you can reach your goals, you have to know what they are. In Alvin's case, he discovered that he did want to become successful, but not at the expense of turning into his father. As soon as he realized that it was this fear of becoming his father that kept him from being successful, he knew that he wasn't being fair to himself. Being successful does not mean being cruel. He knew that he could be successful and also be himself. At the end of our second meeting, Alvin told me that he no longer wanted to be at the mercy of his childhood experience; he wanted to be in control of his life. He wanted to become successful, truly successful. In chapter 5, we'll take a look at exactly how Alvin went about realizing his dreams of success.

The origin of inner conflict

Both my story and Alvin's story reveal how much of our behavior can be determined by our childhood experience. To a great extent the messages we received as children determine our basic beliefs about the world. As children we are a ready audience, but not an informed one. What we were shown, or told, is what we believe. For example, by watching his father, Alvin grew up believing that in order to be successful you had to be cruel. I grew up believing something similar because of what my father told me. As children, we don't have the wisdom to realize that what we learn is not always true. Only as an adult can we unlearn the lesson. Both Alvin and I were in our middle 30s by the time we realized that being successful didn't have to mean being cruel. The problem is, we don't always know what messages we picked up as children. Nonetheless, those messages often subconsciously affect our behavior as adults.

How to achieve your goals of success

In this chapter, I have shown you that before you can achieve success, you must be clear about what you want. In some cases you may have to resolve inner conflicts that are preventing you from becoming successful. The best way to find out whether or not you have any such inner conflicts is to watch your behavior. Are you acting in a way that is consistent with your stated desire to become a success? Are you doing anything that undermines your efforts to achieve your goals? If you discover that you are, you then have to ask yourself why. You may find that the answer lies in the messages you received as a child. You may be able to resolve your inner conflict on your own, or you may, like Alvin, wish to seek some help. However you deal with your issues, you will need to stop doing the things that are sabotaging your efforts. You will need to change your behavior in order to succeed. And that brings us to the 8 Best Practices of high-performing salespeople, because these are the very practices that you can use to realize your dreams of success.

*Most of the low-performing
salespeople spend more time
planning their vacations,
than planning their careers.*

Chapter 3

Best Practice Number 1: Develop and utilize a marketing plan

Once you are clear that you want to become a high-performing salesperson you are ready to put into action the first best practice — develop and utilize a marketing plan.

Success is rarely an accident

Success is rarely an accident. Most of the time, success is the result of developing a plan and utilizing it. In fact, all the high-performing salespeople I have met throughout my many years as a sales trainer have used and continue to use a planning process. In contrast, most of the low-performing salespeople spend more time planning their vacations, than planning their careers. In this chapter, I'll show you how you can develop and utilize a marketing plan, and how that plan will take you to new levels of success. The planning process we'll be looking at involves the following five strategies: 1) Identify your ideal client. 2) Analyze your natural market. 3) Identify your target markets. 4) Prepare your top 20 list. 5) Promote yourself. By following these five strategies, you'll be performing the first best practice of high-performing salespeople.

I'd like to begin this chapter with another story from Tony's career. The event that I am about to describe took place a few years after Tony's meeting with Ivan Kapeck. It is a wonderful example of how exciting your career can be when you develop a marketing plan and utilize it.

Above top secret

A choppy expanse of deep black water stretched ahead of the prow of the motorboat. The tree-lined, far shore of Lake Ranier was barely visible in the distance. Tony Henderson sat rigidly in a small seat at the front of the boat, tightly hugging his briefcase to his chest as spray from the waves splashed up on his suit. Behind him a young man in a white, nautical-looking uniform was piloting the mahogany and brass motorboat. Ahead of him, Tony could see a huge yacht bobbing at anchor in the two-foot swells. It dwarfed their 20 footer. It was the biggest boat he had ever seen on this lake, probably over 60 feet long. His knuckles turned white as he tightened his grip on his briefcase. He hoped that his man would be on board.

As the motorboat drew closer to the massive yacht, Tony noticed that there was nobody on deck. The boat was silent except for the metallic clanging of the anchor line against the hull. He had heard rumors of an inner circle that held clandestine meetings every month out here in the middle of the lake. The rumors said that attendance at these meetings was strictly controlled — exclusive and ultra-secretive. No one he had spoken to really knew who belonged to the group that held the meetings. But everyone said that some of the wealthiest people in town made regular trips out to that boat. He had been digging and digging for months, asking everyone if they had heard about the meetings, if they knew who attended, and what they did.

Finally, last week he discovered that one of his existing clients, a young accountant named Brian Treble, had an in with the group. His father, the CEO of Mexicala Rio, a local restaurant chain, was a member of the mysterious star chamber. Brian arranged a meeting between Tony and his dad. Over dinner, Mr. Treble was evasive when Tony asked him about the yacht. He tried to downplay the rumors that Tony had heard, tersely assuring him that the mystery was really quite overblown. They were only a group of CEOs that needed a place to meet that was safe from prying eyes. It still seemed strange to Tony.

Inevitably, the dinner conversation turned to business. As it turned out, Brian's father was a regular reader of Tony's weekly column on mutual fund investing in the local business paper. Mr. Treble liked what Tony had to say and had actually used several of his tips to manage his own investments. On the strength of that connection Tony managed to work his way onto the group's agenda.

He only had twenty minutes to make his presentation, but he knew it would be long enough for the group to decide whether to support him or not. His biggest worry was whether the one man he wanted to meet would be there.

As the motorboat approached the bow of the massive yacht, the young man behind Tony cut the engine and slid smoothly alongside. Tony saw a hatch open and two men come out. A folding metal staircase was lowered from the deck of the yacht and Tony saw Mr. Treble waiting at the top. Still unsure of his footing in the light waves, Tony managed to make his way nervously up the stairs. At the top, he stepped out onto the long flat deck of the yacht, smiled and thrust out a hand to greet Mr. Treble.

"Whew," he said, "I'm glad I made it. I'm not really very comfortable on the water. Luckily, this boat's big enough that I don't think I have to worry about falling over the side."

"Yes, I'd say you're pretty safe, son," said Treble, letting go of his hand and turning to walk away. "Follow me, we're ready for you now."

Treble wasn't the friendliest man Tony had ever met, even if he was Brian's father. His brusque demeanor didn't do much to soothe Tony's nerves. They walked through a hatch and Tony found himself in a narrow corridor leading deeper into the ship. The walls were lined with dark wood, paintings of ancient schooners and storm-tossed coastlines were hung at regular intervals, burgundy carpet was laid out underfoot. The ship seemed to breathe wealth. Everything about it was expensive.

After a few minutes of walking down similar hallways, turning a seemingly endless series of corners, and navigating steeply angled stairs, Tony found himself completely disoriented. He wasn't sure if it was the owner's intention, but he had no idea where he was — except that he was deep within the bowels of the ship. Eventually, they came upon a large doorway filled by two heavy oak doors with large ornate handles. Mr. Treble pushed them open and walked through. When he saw the gargantuan circular table that dominated the room and the dozen or so deeply lined and tanned faces that surrounded it, Tony's heart began to pound. He had penetrated the inner circle. Anxiously he looked around for the face of the one man he was here to speak to.

Tony's stomach churned. He didn't see him. The man he had worked so hard to meet wasn't one of the 13 seated around the table. Tony quickly scanned the rest of the room, large ferns stood in the corners, portholes lined one wall, a few chairs and coffee tables were arranged behind the big meeting table. Suddenly, Tony's eyes widened. His flagging spirits soared. There, behind the group already seated around the polished wooden table, a slight, odd-looking man in a blue suit sat hunched over a pile of papers. Tony immediately recognized him from the pictures in the newspapers. He was Tony's ideal vision of a client — Sam Garroffolo, the steel mill magnate. Most likely the richest man in the room.

Mr. Treble took one of the empty seats beside his cohorts and motioned silently for Tony to step up to the small wooden podium at the head of the table. As he took his notes out of his briefcase and arranged them on the podium, Tony's hands shook. He hoped the people at the table couldn't tell.

As Tony finished ordering his papers, he looked more closely at the men and women in front of him. He did recognize a few of them. To his left was Lomar Itrescu, who owned Yogie!, the diet ice cream company. To his right sat Bill Withers and Steve Randle, the inseparable friends who, respectively, owned the magnificent golf course over on Spider Lake and the Aquaworld amusement park in Chatham. And behind them was Judy Wu, who had started a herbal medicines company in her basement and built it into a global corporation.

He had seen a lot of these faces in the local papers and in trade journals. But he still didn't know exactly why they met on the first Tuesday of every month. He guessed that decisions were made within these four walls, on this yacht, that would have a significant impact on the local economy. These were the elite of the local business community. Tony hoped they would appreciate the ideas and information he had for them. And, if he could gain their trust and support, his career would definitely move to a new level. But, in truth, when he planned this talk, he had focused his research efforts on their most prominent member. He had created this speech with Sam Garroffolo in mind.

Tony spoke for the next twenty minutes on "Diversifying your personal wealth." His audience listened in silence. As he spoke his level of unease grew. They gave him no indication of what they thought about the concepts he was proposing. Finally, he reached the end of his talk. He paused and said, "I hope that has helped you to understand the importance of diversifying your personal wealth outside of your businesses. I would like to thank you all for allowing me to speak to you today. And I would especially like to thank Mr. Treble for all of his help. But before I leave, does anyone have any questions?"

Tony scanned the faces around the room, but nobody said anything. He still couldn't tell what they thought of his presentation. Shuffling his papers into order and reaching for his briefcase, he said, "Okay then, thanks again. I'll leave copies of my presentation and business cards in case any of you have questions later."

As Tony packed up his materials, several of the people got up from the table and left the room. Two others pulled out cellular phones and began talking softly as they paced the room. Tony closed his briefcase and spun the dials to lock it. Glancing up, he saw Mr. Treble standing beside him waiting to take him back to the motorboat.

"Thanks, Tony," Mr. Treble said. "I'm sure your information will be put to good use. I know I heard some things I hadn't really considered before."

As he picked up his briefcase, Tony desperately scanned the room one last time. He had come all this way, his speech had gone off without a hitch, but he still hadn't done what he set out to do — meet Sam Garroffolo. He looked over at the chair in the corner where Mr. Garroffolo had remained seated throughout the entire talk, but he was no longer there. Tony grimaced with disappointment.

"Thanks, Mr. Treble," he said, reaching out his hand. "I guess I'll be going then." They shook hands, this time more warmly than when Tony had first arrived. Mr. Treble smiled and walked past Tony towards the door. Tony turned to follow but almost tripped over the small man who had been standing right behind him. It was Mr. Garroffolo.

Mr. Garroffolo's thin face cracked open into a lopsided grin. "Son," he said, "nice work. I'm Sam Garroffolo, I own the steel mill in Norfolk and a few others besides and I like what you had to say today."

"Thanks!" said Tony, shaking the man's rough hand.

Mr. Garroffolo nodded and then began to walk away. "Call my secretary next Tuesday," he said, grinning over his shoulder as he returned to his chair in the corner. "We need to talk."

Tony called on schedule, and within a few weeks he had added Sam Garroffolo to his roster of clients. Tony was thrilled. Having Sam as his client was the culmination of something he had begun years ago — developing and utilizing a marketing plan. Now I'd like to take you back nine years ago to the first meeting I had with Tony and explore how we got Tony started on the first best practice of high-performing salespeople.

Tony: the journey begins

I pulled my 4 x 4 into an empty parking spot in the gravel lot behind an old brick building on Mortimer Ave. I had driven almost two hours, across bumpy highway and unfinished back roads to get here. For once I was glad I had an off-road vehicle, usually it didn't get much more of a work out than hauling our family's groceries on a Saturday afternoon.

I grabbed my briefcase from the rear seat and went inside. Checking my watch I saw that I was right on time for my 11 o'clock meeting with Tony. This would be our first one-on-one meeting. Tony had attended a seminar I delivered to a group of salespeople, and called me afterwards for some private consultation because he wanted to find a way to increase his income.

I walked through the glass front doors of the building and up two flights of stairs to reach his office. The door was open and I could see Tony sitting alone behind a desk in the small room. He had no secretary, and was talking excitedly into the phone when I stopped in the doorway. Tony looked up from his desk, acknowledged me with raised eyebrows, then covered the mouthpiece of his phone and whispered, "Norm, hi. Come on in. I'll just be a second."

I sat down across the desk from him and waited while he resumed his telephone conversation. He had his tie loosened and the top button of his shirt was undone, and I noticed he was sweating even though cool air was blowing in from his open window.

I didn't want to pry, but I couldn't help but hear Tony's end of the conversation.

"There is no question you should start buying mutual funds, Rick," Tony said. "The earlier you start on your retirement planning, the more wealth you will have accumulated by the time you're 65. Let me put it this way, Rick. You're 30 now. If you start putting away even $2,000 a year and average, let's say 8%, by the time you come to retire, you'll have over $315,000. That's amazing considering you're only going to be putting in $66,000."

Tony stopped and listened to Rick. He nodded and grunted into the phone. His mouth curled into a grimace.

"Rick, I know, man," he said. "I'm just trying to help you out. This really is something you need. You have a family now."

I sat there for another few minutes, patiently waiting for Tony to finish. Every now and then he would cover the mouthpiece, sigh, roll his eyes at me, and then give me an apologetic look.

Tony seemed to be one of those people who is constantly run off his feet, scrambling to keep up with an unrelenting work pace. My guess was Tony was working hard, but not smart. A lot of people working 60 hours a week could accomplish much more in half the time, if they knew how to work more efficiently. And you can only do that if you have a plan. I could tell by how frustrated Tony appeared that we would be focusing our energies today on developing a marketing plan for him.

At last, Tony said, with a resigned tone in his voice, "No. No. Okay, sure. Yeah, okay, Rick. That's fine. Look, we'll keep in touch, right. I'll call you again in a couple of months. Okay, say hi to Beth for me. See ya later."

He put the receiver back into the cradle and blew a long sigh out of his mouth as he pushed his hair off his sweaty forehead.

"Hi, Norm," he said, reaching over the desk to shake my hand. "Whew, I just can't believe how hard it is to sell some of these people. I'm beginning to think I need your help more than I thought."

"How do you mean, Tony?" I asked.

"Well, that guy was a friend of mine in high school. He can trust me. I'm not trying to rip him off. He's got a wife and a 2-year-old girl. He really does need to start planning for their future. All I'm asking is that he put $2,000 in a mutual fund, and he can't even do that."

"Hmmmm. Well, let's see what we can do for you, then." I replied.

Our first step would be to try to identify what Tony's goals were. You can't develop a plan without knowing what the plan is supposed to achieve. And remember, we saw in chapter 2 that you can't become successful unless you truly want to be.

"Tony," I started, "I want to ask you what prompted you to call me last week and set up this meeting?"

"I know William Spence and Barb Cuppolo, and both of them say you've helped them get to where they are now. I want you to help me the way you helped them."

"Can you tell me what you made last year, Tony?" I asked.

"Sure — $60,000. I think that's pretty good, but I'd like to do better."

"How much better?"

"I'd like to make a hundred grand next year, Norm."

"Is that it?" I asked.

"Yeah, that's my goal."

"Okay, but what about beyond that?"

"You mean, what do I want to do with the rest of my life?"

"Sure."

"Well, I'd like to stay in this business. I think it's something I could really be good at."

"And would you be happy making $100,000 a year ten years from now?"

"No, I guess not. By then I'd like to be financially independent."

"And what would it take for you to be financially independent?"

"Making a million dollars a year," Tony exclaimed.

I was glad that Tony was able to clearly express what he wanted. Whatever plan we developed would have to help him achieve his goals.

"Tony, how were you planning on eventually reaching an annual income of $1 million a year?"

"I don't really know. All I know is I'm working damn hard now, and if you're going to tell me to work harder, I'm not really sure I can do that. I already work 6, sometimes 7 days a week, and often 12 hours a day."

Working way too hard

"Well, I can tell you I'm not going to be asking you to work harder, that's for sure. So don't worry about that. Before we figure out what you should be doing, why don't you tell me what you're doing right now."

"You mean how I'm working?" Tony asked.

"Yes."

"Well, right now I have about 180 clients who I call on a regular basis. It's taken me three years to build that up — working like a dog."

"And what are your clients like? I heard you on the phone when I came in. It sounded like you were talking to one of your clients. Is he pretty typical of your clientele, Tony?"

"Well, not all of them, but probably the majority of them are professionals like him. They make good money. They're young, around my age. I think they are a good market."

"You're right — they are. But you need more than just one market, Tony," I said. "They're a good market for someone who wants to continue making $60,000 a year, but you'll need to develop other markets if you're going to make $100,000 next year, and eventually $1 million. Let me put it to you this way, Tony. You made $60,000 off 180 clients last year. That's a lot of effort. You made an average of $333 per client. You'd need another 120 clients to reach $100,000 at that rate. And to reach a million dollars, you'd need 3,000 clients. I don't think you have enough hours in the day to see all those people."

Tony looked embarrassed. I wasn't trying to be harsh. I just wanted him to see the problem in the proper terms.

"I guess my hope was I'd grow with them as their careers matured and their incomes grew," he said sheepishly.

"But that will take time, and from what you've told me, you don't have that kind of time. You want to make $100,000 as soon as next year. I doubt that your market is going to grow that quickly. Besides, why would you want your career to depend on whether or not the people in your market get rich sometime in the future. Certainly some will, but some won't."

"So what do I do?" Tony asked, sounding helpless.

"You change the way you work," I replied.

"But how?"

"You have to figure out a way of working so that you can easily make $100,000 next year, and eventually have a $1-million annual income."

"And how do I figure out what to do?" Tony asked.

"Simple — you develop a marketing plan, and utilize it."

Strategy 1: Identify your ideal client

"The first strategy in developing and utilizing a marketing plan is to determine who your ideal client would be. Tony, you're obviously frustrated selling to your current crop of prospects and we've established that they aren't going to get you to your goal. So, who would you like to be selling to? Who would you rather be spending your time with?"

"Umm, well, people who have more money than my current prospects, I guess," Tony said.

"Right. But, in order to build the marketing plan, we need a clear picture of the types of people you will be selling to."

Tony looked worried. "Norm," he said, "you seem to have this all figured out. Who do *you* think I should be selling to. What's a hot market right now?"

I laughed, politely. "Tony, I wish I could give you a simple answer to that question. Believe me, it would make me a very popular consultant. But, everyone has a different answer to that question because there is no one ideal client for all salespeople. I can't tell you that you should be selling to doctors — you might not want to work with them, and maybe you don't have the right personality or skills to sell to them. Forcing yourself to sell to a market you have absolutely no connection to is not the best practice. You have to figure out where your talents and interests lie."

Demographics and Psychographics

"Okay, so how specific should I be when I describe my ideal client?" Tony asked.

"You should be able to describe them in terms of their demographics and psychographics. Demographics are how you describe someone statistically — age, income, education, things like that. Psychographics are how you describe someone's values, needs, wants, beliefs, attitudes. For example, Tony, demographically, I would probably describe the people you are selling to now as 25 to 35-year-old, married, college-educated professionals making an income in excess of $40,000 a year. Psychographically, these people are in a consumer mode, spending a lot of money on things like appliances, furniture, cars, a mortgage or rent. They want a lot, but at the same time they're trying to make sure they save a little and don't go too heavily into debt."

"Sounds pretty close to me," said Tony.

The rich folk of Simcoe Hall

"So," I asked, "let's start by describing your ideal client demographically. Who are they? What do they do? What age are they?"

"Well, they should be older than the people I'm selling to now. Instead of just starting out in their career, they should already be established. They're probably in their late 50s or older, and wealthy by now — earning a six-figure income, with a seven-figure net worth."

"Okay," I said, "let's see if we can get an even clearer picture of these people. Who are you seeing in your head when you talk about these older people? Do you know anyone like that right now?"

"Well, there's the older men and women who hang out at Simcoe Hall. That's the big resort on Lake Ranier. You know, the place where you can dock your boat at the bar. They've got tennis courts and a private golf course. I think there's a spa in there as well."

I'd been to Simcoe Hall myself. It was a beautiful place. A sprawling resort on one of the finest lakes in cottage country. It was a habitual haunt for the local elite and their families. I knew that the people who stayed there would be perfect prospects if you were trying to make $1 million a year.

"And can you describe these people psychographically, Tony?" I asked.

"Well, they're older, closing in on their retirement years, so they know they only have a few years left to build up their retirement nest egg. I think their aggressive consumer years are probably over — they probably have most of the things they want materially — a home, a cottage, a couple of cars, nice furniture, an art collection, that kind of stuff. If they haven't already, they're trying to pay off all their debts. They're starting to save heavily, and they want some good growth."

"That's good, Tony," I said. "I think you've developed a pretty good picture of your ideal client. The thing to remember is your ideal client becomes the focus of your marketing plan. Your plan must get you to the point where you are selling to your ideal client, as well as your current prospects."

"But how exactly am I going to get to these ideal clients?" Tony asked. "I'm not selling to any of them now."

"Don't worry, Tony. We'll find a way. In fact, that's what we're going to do right now. Let's turn to the second strategy."

Tony leaned forward with interest.

Strategy 2: Analyze your natural market

"Okay, Tony," I said, "now we're going to analyze your natural market — you'll see why we're doing this in a moment. Your natural market is made up of your clients, the prospects you are currently approaching, and the people you know, such as family, friends, acquaintances. In other words, your natural market is your network."

We spent the next few minutes discussing the people that made up Tony's natural market. In the end, we discovered that the 25 to 35-year-old professionals we discussed earlier made up about 70% of Tony's natural market. Another 20% included a small group of small business owners between the ages of 35 and 55. The rest was family, and a handful of friends and acquaintances.

"You see," said Tony, "not a single ideal client in there."

"Tony, the reason we are analyzing your natural market is because we are going to use it as a tool to get to your ideal client. There's no point starting from scratch, you have to use what you have. We have to find a way to use your natural market as a springboard to your ideal client."

"Oh, I see," said Tony.

"Let me ask you, of all the people we have looked at in your natural market, do any of them know someone who might be an ideal client for you?"

Tony glanced up at the ceiling, thought for a few moments, then said, "Well, many of the young professionals I sell to have parents that own successful businesses and hang out at Simcoe Hall."

"Well, then, Tony, there you go. That's how you can get to your ideal client. Instead of just selling to one of your peers, you're also trying to gain an introduction to their parents."

Tony nodded.

"This brings us to the next strategy in developing your marketing plan — identify your target markets.

Strategy 3: Identify your target markets

"Your ideal clients are people 55 years old and above who are affluent, meaning that they are making more than $100,000 a year, and have a net worth of over $1 million. That should definitely be your first target market."

"I see," said Tony. "And what about other target markets in my natural market?"

"As we said, you will definitely need more than one market. You will need a number of markets that are distinct and serve a number of purposes. You won't be able to reach your goal of $100,000 next year concentrating solely on your ideal clients. You won't be able to walk in tomorrow and sell many of them. It will take some time to cultivate that market. What you need to do is find another worthwhile market to target as a way of sustaining and growing your income over the short-term. . . . Identifying target markets is the key to leveraging your natural market. You need a cluster of robust marketing strategies. You have to look at which clusters of people in your natural market you should target so that eventually you'll be able to reach your ideal client. You should continue to target and sell to 25 to 35-year-old professionals. But, let me ask you, Tony, who in your natural market are you making most of your money from now?"

"From the 35 to 55-year-old small business owners, for sure," Tony replied. "They're older and have more money to save. I bet most of my income comes from them."

"Yet they only make up 20% of your natural market, Tony."

"I know," Tony said, regretfully.

The rule of 80/20

"Actually, Tony," I said, "your situation is very common. A lot of salespeople make 80% of their money from 20% of their clientele, and 20% of their income from 80% of their clientele. Of course, what you should be doing is flipping that around. You should spend

80% of your time working the small portion of your natural market that makes you money, until eventually that portion grows from 20% to 80%."

"So, if I concentrate on the three target markets we just discussed — the affluent Simcoe Hall crowd that is 55 plus, their children who are 25 to 35, and the 35 to 55-year-old business owners — what do I do with the rest of my market? Throw them out? Some of them are friends and they all bring in money in some small degree."

The transition plan

"No, don't just dump them," I replied. "Don't forget that your marketing plan is a method for migrating your business from where it is today to where you want it to be tomorrow. It's not an instantaneous process at all. There will be a transition period where you still deal with non-ideal clients. But you should start focusing right now on your target markets. That's where your future growth will come from.

Draw a line in your natural market

"Tony, 35% of the calls most salespeople make are to poor prospects — people who will never buy, or if they do buy are going to cancel shortly after. There's no reason for this waste of time. Remember, one of the advantages of being a salesperson is that you can choose who you want to work with. What you have to do is draw a line in your natural market — a line below which you won't sell. If a prospect doesn't approximate the demographic and psychographic profile for your ideal client or doesn't belong in one of your target markets, you have to evaluate whether it's worth spending your time on them. Wouldn't you be better off using that time to call on someone from your target markets or trying to get an appointment with an ideal client?

Strategy 4: Prepare your top 20 list

"After drawing a line in your natural market and determining who you won't sell to, you should then try and figure out who in your natural market you should be focusing on. An effective way of doing that is to create a list of the 20 most important relationships you have within that market. Your most important relationships are not necessarily clients — they may be potential clients or centers of influence. Then, for each person on the list, identify their income and net worth."

Tony knew his top 20 relationships immediately, so it only took him a few minutes to jot their names and financial stats down.

"Okay, let's add up those figures," I said. "What are those 20 people worth?"

"Their net worth is. . . ," Tony paused while he did the arithmetic on his calculator, "$300,000 on average. But their total net worth as a group is $6 million. Wow, that's a lot! I don't think the total net worth of all of my clients is even $8 million."

"That's not surprising," I said. "You'll probably find that those 20 represent a huge percentage of your income. In fact, studies of the top sales professionals in the financial services industry indicate that 80% or more of the salesperson's business comes from 20 important relationships. That's where you should focus your energy.

"But that's not all," I continued. "Because 'like breeds like' each of those 20 people probably know 20 people with a similar financial status. Which means that if you broaden your network to include their networks, we're talking about a total net worth of $126 million. You see, you have your original network of 20 clients, plus an additional 20 networks of 20."

I saw Tony's eyes widen.

"And," I continued, "those 20 people know another 20 who in turn know another 20. . . . So if you concentrate on those first 20 most important relationships you can see how easy it is to build up a lot of very wealthy clients very quickly — it's targeted networking.

"Once you've figured out your target markets, and picked your top 20, your next challenge is to figure out a way to drill deep into those markets. And that takes us to the last strategy of developing and utilizing a marketing plan — promote yourself.

Strategy 5: Promote yourself

"Tony, this strategy is crucial because it is the 'utilize' part of this first best practice. If you complete the first four strategies and forget to do the last one, you'll actually get nowhere. You need to promote yourself to your target markets and to your ideal client so that you can build up those markets to the point where they make up 80% of your clientele."

"How do I do that?" Tony asked.

"Let me ask you if you have done anything to promote yourself already?"

"I've written a few articles on mutual funds in the local community newspaper and last year I teamed up with another salesperson and we held a mutual fund seminar. I got a few clients from that."

"Well, you're on the right track, then," I said. "But you should start doing more of it, and make sure that your promotion is directed at your target markets, and your ideal client. For example, instead of writing about mutual funds in general, why not do a series on the specific benefits of mutual funds to the small business owner?"

"Good idea!" Tony exclaimed, pointing at me with his pen. "I'm definitely going to do that. And I could do seminars that target retirement issues and attract those 55 plus affluent prospects."

"That's right," I replied. "You must develop some expertise in solving the specific problems of your target markets. And you should present yourself to them as an expert. You want your target market to realize that they need you. In other words, Tony, promotion is first about telling your target markets that you exist, and second, about telling them how you can help them."

Tony and I spent the next few minutes coming up with other ways he could promote himself. On top of writing articles and giving seminars, we discussed how Tony could also promote himself through personal introductions, advertising in magazines, newspapers and on the radio.

The plan in action

At the end of our meeting, I could tell that Tony was excited and eager to put his plan into action. In the weeks and months that followed, Tony executed a massive promotional campaign.

Right away, he began asking his peers — the young professionals — for introductions to their parents. In fact, this was how he managed to get his first appointment with an ideal client — he asked his friend John to help get him a meeting with his father, Ivan

Kapeck, the multimillionaire we met in chapter 1.

Tony also began arranging and booking seminars. He purchased mailing lists that included people who fit his target markets and his ideal client profile. For example, he bought a list of people who owned homes in an affluent neighborhood. He would send each person on the list a letter telling them about an upcoming seminar in their neighborhood, and then he followed up with calls from a telemarketer. He was careful to make sure the seminar would be of interest to his audience, and avoided making the seminar sound like an infomercial. He wanted to give his prospects information and advice they could take away; he wanted them to value his advice and expertise.

One type of seminar he liked to give was a breakfast seminar for business owners. Over a period of a few months, he delivered half a dozen breakfast seminars on topics like succession planning, and how business owners could transfer a business to their children, their employees, or to a third party. He also hosted a number of seminars — rather than delivering them himself — on topics such as employee compensation and employee benefits. For those he brought in outside experts. His reputation as someone who could help business owners began to spread and soar.

One ingenious way Tony began to promote himself was to team up with a mutual fund management company to run 60-second spots on the radio. The company sponsored the spots in which Tony offered his tips and advice on retirement planning and investment management.

Tony also continued to write many articles for magazines and newspapers, and ran ads in those publications.

The payoff

Tony's promotion paid off. A year later his income was over his target of $100,000. But that was just the beginning. Tony continued to grow his business at a very rapid rate.

In the dramatic scene that took place on the yacht in the middle of Lake Ranier, we saw that Tony had to use all five strategies I have outlined in this chapter to win Sam Garroffolo's confidence. He had defined his ideal client and found that Mr. Garroffolo fit that profile perfectly. Then Tony analyzed his natural market and found that he could get to Mr. Garroffolo through an existing client of his, Brian Treble. Because Mr. Garroffolo was part of Tony's target market, he knew he could give a presentation that would appeal to him. All of Tony's promotional events and activities were directed at his target markets. For instance, the articles he had written for the local business papers had built up Mr. Treble's confidence in him to the point where he was willing to invite Tony to a meeting on the yacht.

Eventually, Tony also realized his dream of making a million dollars in one year. Today, nine years after our first meeting, Tony spends close to 80% of his time selling only to people who fit his ideal client profile — wealthy business owners 55 years plus — and his yearly income is in excess of $2 million. He is, by his own definition, financially independent.

The snake eats its tail

One last thing to keep in mind about developing and utilizing a marketing plan is that you must be constantly reviewing and revising your plan. As your business grows and your ideal client changes, you will need to adjust your marketing plan accordingly. A marketing plan is not a dead artifact that is so inflexible that it cannot accommodate change. For example, Tony was constantly adjusting his plan as he grew over the years. The line he drew in his natural market kept rising, and he gradually spent less and less time on prospects that didn't fit his ideal. This is why Tony now spends most of his time selling to his ideal client. The purpose of the plan is to make sure you are always heading in the correct direction and taking the shortest possible route to your goals. Tony wanted to keep increasing his income, and so he had to constantly revisit his plan. As Winston Churchill once said, "Plans are useless and planning is invaluable."

Best Practice Number 1: Develop and utilize a marketing plan

1) Identify your ideal client.
2) Analyze your natural market.
3) Identify your target markets.
4) Prepare your top 20 list.
5) Promote yourself.

Mr. Mortone sat back
in his chair and brought the tips
of the fingers of each hand together
into a pyramid in front of his chest.
He thought for a minute,
his face remaining impassive
— impossible to read.

Chapter 4

Best Practice Number 2:
Know your client ·

Once you are able to obtain appointments with people in your chosen target markets by utilizing the first best practice, your next challenge is to sell them. By using the second best practice — know your client — you will be able to create an environment where selling becomes easier.

In this chapter we'll look at four strategies for knowing your clients: 1) Understand your clients' personal needs. 2) Understand your clients' business issues. 3) Understand your clients' financial risk/return relationships. 4) Prepare, practice and perfect risk/return scripts.

When I use the word 'client' in this chapter to refer to the second best practice or any of the strategies, I am using it to mean your clients as a group, not your clients as individuals. Know your client is about understanding the personal needs, business issues and risk/return relationships of a group of people, specifically the clients in your target markets. Later, when we get to best practices numbers 3 and 4, we'll be exploring the importance of understanding the needs, wants and values of specific individual clients. But, for now, let's see how we can use the knowledge of your target market's characteristics to help you become a high-performing salesperson.

Let's go back to Tony's story, and take a look at how he was able to put this second best practice to use.

Strategy 1: Understand your clients' personal needs

My second meeting with Tony Henderson took place a week after I had first sat down with him to create his marketing plan. We agreed to meet at his office at 10 o'clock in the morning. When I stopped in the doorway to his small office, I noticed the window was open and a cool, late summer breeze was blowing through. Unlike the first time I met Tony, his office was quiet — the phone was on it's cradle and he had his head down, busily writing on a stack of papers in front of him. It seemed that our efforts to streamline his work habits and focus his attention on the clients that count were already paying off. He no longer seemed so frantic and frustrated.

I stepped through the door and said, "Tony, hello, how are you?"

Tony looked up when he heard my voice. "Hi, Norm," he said, standing and reaching across his desk to shake my hand. "I was just working on an article for the Bayshore Gazette. It's called 'Retire without worry.'"

"That's great," I said, sitting down across from him. "It's good to see that you've taken the first best practice to heart and have put it into action already."

"Well, I'm excited about freeing up my time and making more money. I want to start as soon as possible."

"Well, the first best practice will allow you to create lots of opportunity, but now we have to make sure that you can take advantage of those opportunities. We should get started on best practice number 2 — know your client."

"Okay," Tony responded.

"Our objective here is to make sure you get to know the personal needs of the people in your target markets, because it is those people you want as clients. We began talking about personal needs last week when we discussed demographics and psychographics. Let's further explore personal needs by going over something that I refer to as the three phases of financial management.

The three phases of financial management

"Tony, as people age they pass through three very distinct phases. It is crucial for all financial salespeople to be familiar with these phases.

Phase 1: Age 20-40 — cash flow management

"Phase 1 is made up of those people between the ages of 20 and 40. You'll notice that most of your natural market is in this phase, and you are probably well acquainted with the personal needs of these people. They are primarily concerned with cash flow management, which includes asset and income protection. They spend most of their money paying the bills, and taking care of the basics. With whatever money is left over, and with whatever credit they have, they acquire material goods such as stereos, barbecues, cars, homes.

Phase 2: Age 40-60 — asset accumulation

"Phase 2 is made up of people aged 40 to 60. This is the phase where a good portion of your combined target markets lies. These people are primarily concerned with asset accumulation. They need a financial plan which helps them minimize taxes. They also need to diversify their investments to protect themselves from losses. They can't afford to take fantastic risks with speculative stocks and funds like they did when they were young because they don't have the time to recoup losses before retirement. But they do need to maximize their return on whatever investments they have. They aren't retired yet and they still have time to increase the amount of capital they will have available when they retire. They need to ensure that they will have a good income waiting for them when they step away from their business.

Phase 3: Age 60 plus — asset management and utilization

"Phase 3 typically includes anyone 60 years and older. These people are primarily concerned with asset management and utilization. They need a financial plan that manages their budget, has an insurance component to offset estate taxes and makes allowances for lump sum investments into mutual funds and annuities, so that they will have income in their retirement years."

Tony nodded after I outlined the three phases.

"If you can understand these three phases, Tony, you'll have a good grounding in knowing your client. The point is, you don't want to be approaching someone who is over 60, as though they were 30. But there's more to knowing your client than simply knowing what phase they are in and what their personal needs are. You must also understand their business issues, which is the second strategy in knowing your client.

Strategy 2: Understand your clients' business issues

"In order to fully understand your clients' business issues you have to completely immerse yourself in that market. Think about the things you already do to understand your current clients' businesses. How do you know what they are concerned with?"

"Ummm," Tony responded, "since most of them are my friends, I hear a lot of their gripes and problems just by speaking to them, to be honest." he said.

"That's good," I reassured him. "If you can, that's exactly how you should get that information."

"Yeah. People love to talk about themselves and their businesses," he observed.

"So, what would you do if you needed to find out about your ideal client's business?"

Immerse yourself in their world

Tony took a moment to watch the street scene outside the window before answering. "Since they are older people, I'd have to change my behavior. Instead of going to Alfred's for lunch and eating with friends, I'd make sure I was getting lunch appointments with my friends and their parents. Then I would just do the same thing I do now — ask them about their business and listen carefully to what they have to tell me.

Socialize

"I know they spend a lot of their recreational time at places like Simcoe Hall — so I'd become a member there. I'd play a lot more tennis and golf than I do now, just so I could meet them in a more social environment. I find it's always easier to get people talking about themselves and their businesses when they're relaxed and their guard is down."

"So, what you're telling me is that you'd immerse yourself in their world, is that right?" I asked.

"Yes," he said, nodding.

"Apart from social engagements then, how else could you immerse yourself in their world?"

Trade journals

Tony looked around his office as if searching for inspiration. "With my clients right now," he said, "a lot of them are professionals — lawyers and doctors — so I get some of the journals that their associations put out. That helps me to keep up with the latest news in their industry. Hopefully, I know as soon as they do if new businesses are opening up, or if legal issues that concern them arise. I can also find out things like who is being made partner somewhere, or what doctor is opening up a clinic. I guess I would have to do this kind of research for my ideal clients."

Join their associations

"Yes," I said, "studying their journals and magazines is an excellent way to learn about your clients' business issues. If you are going to completely understand what concerns they share you need to get their trade journals because that's one important way they communicate with each other. But also, consider the other ways that people within an industry communicate. Why not actually join their trade associations if possible. Certainly attend their seminars, workshops and conferences. That'll give you a chance to meet a lot of the players in the business in person.

Use what you already know

"Also, look at your current clients in your natural market. Some of your prospects may be fairly close to your ideal client in terms of demographics and psychographics. They may even be in the same business, just different ages or income levels."

"So," Tony said, "you're suggesting that I could transfer knowledge about my current clients' business issues to my ideal clients. I do already have a few clients who are older than me and who own and manage their own businesses. I could see if any of their issues would apply to my ideal clients."

Applying strategies 1 and 2 to the Ivan Kapeck deal

Tony would eventually capitalize on the idea of using what you already know — that was how he sold Ivan Kapeck, Tony's first multimillionaire client who we met in chapter 1. Tony knew what business issues would concern Ivan Kapeck, because he knew that Ivan would share one crucial similarity with the business owners he was already familiar with — their lack of time to manage their personal finances with the same energy they manage their business.

Tony also understood that Ivan Kapeck would share other key similarities with the business owners in his market. He knew, for instance, that Ivan would be concerned about managing the risks inherent in his business. And, as we saw in chapter 1, Tony was able to impress Ivan with his understanding of liability and risk, and how diversifying investments could be used to mitigate the risks of a business.

Tony was also aware which financial management phase Ivan fell into. He knew that, because Ivan was 56, he was in the late stages of phase 2 and would be concerned with asset accumulation and making sure he had enough money to live on when retired.

By knowing all these things about Ivan — his personal needs and his business issues — even before meeting him, Tony set the stage for making the sale.

Strategy 3: Understand your clients' financial risk/return relationships

Once you understand your clients' personal needs and business issues, you will be able to begin constructing a picture of their financial risk/return relationships. You should compare all the losses your clients are exposed to against all the returns they have the potential to make — both personally and in their businesses. You will now have a valuable head start even before seeing a particular prospect. Because you understand what their risks and returns are, you won't have to start from scratch in your first meeting with them and waste precious time with basic questions. Let's take a look at how Tony was able to use this strategy to help him make an immediate impact in a challenging case. This story involves a prospect Tony met shortly after he gained Ivan Kapeck as a client.

If the shoe fits

The elevator doors opened and Tony walked through into the lobby of Mortone Enterprises. A secretary sat at a desk to his right and to his left a large oak door was framed by two potted palms. He was a couple of minutes early for his meeting with Carlos Mortone so he took a seat to wait until the secretary called him. As he waited he went back over the details of the case.

Mortone was the father of Raul, one of Tony's clients. At age 62, Mortone was close to retirement and from what Tony had been able to find out from Raul, most of Mortone's money was still tied up in the business. The office he was sitting in now employed about 35 people and was responsible for the operation of a chain of 20 shoe stores. They did about $15 million a year and the business was growing rapidly. Tony knew, from Raul, that Carlos still ran the company, and did so 'with an iron fist.' It was typical that the owner of a business of this size would be heavily involved in the day-to-day operations. In fact, the entire family, all of the sons and daughters, were working for Mortone Corp.

Based on his research and his knowledge of his clients in the same target market, Tony had developed what he hoped would be a winning approach to this sale. He felt he understood the business issues facing Carlos and the financial risk/return relationships that he was likely to have. Now he just had to lay them out for his prospect and deliver the solution.

After a few minutes, Mr. Mortone's secretary showed Tony through to Mr. Mortone's office, a spacious corner unit, with a view of the river and the docks below.

Mr. Mortone stood and greeted Tony warmly. "Tony Henderson, nice to meet you," he said, shaking Tony's hand. "My son, Raul, says you're very good."

"Hello, thank you, sir," Tony replied, taking a seat at the desk.

"So, what can I do for you today?" asked Mr. Mortone, straightening a small stack of papers on his immaculate desk. Tony noticed liver spots on the back of his hands as they moved across the white surface of the papers. "I was led to believe that this has something to do with my finances?"

"Yes, sir," Tony began. "Actually, as you know, I handle Raul's finances for him and our plan for his future involves investing and managing a lot of the income he derives from his share of this company."

"Yes, of course," responded Mr. Mortone. "He seems to be doing very well by all counts. Congratulations, Mr. Henderson."

"Well, that's why I'm here today. In the course of determining his financial plan I have learned a lot about Mortone Corp., it's financial picture and it's future. I also have a lot of experience with clients in your situation, and I believe I have a financial opportunity that would interest you, Mr. Mortone."

"So?" asked Mr. Mortone, inclining his head slightly towards Tony. Mortone was Brazilian by birth and still had many of the mannerisms of the old country. He was given to the subtle nods and gestures of a more polite society. Tony took this gesture as a signal to proceed.

"Mr. Mortone," he said, "if we could work together to design *and* implement a plan to guarantee that your personal finances outperform even the profits of this company, ensure your retirement income and also deal with the transfer of your estate after your death would that be of interest to you?"

Mr. Mortone sat back in his chair and brought the tips of the fingers of each hand together into a pyramid in front of his chest. He thought for a minute, his face remaining impassive — impossible to read.

Finally, he said, "Mr. Henderson, you are very direct. But that is okay. We are, after all, in a business meeting, are we not? Tell me more, I am intrigued."

"Mr. Mortone," he said, "I believe I have a good understanding of the problem you face. You are 62 years old. In my experience that means you are likely concerned with planning for your retirement and the transfer of your company to your heirs. From my dealings with other clients, I also know that you are probably very busy with the business. In fact, so busy that you likely don't spend nearly enough time on your personal finances as you should. That's why I would like to propose that I take on a role as your personal financial advisor. If you agree, I will work with you to prepare a plan for diversifying your investments and converting them to annuities and income funds at the proper time." Tony held up a blue folder and opened it so that Mr. Mortone could see the sample plan inside.

He watched Mr. Mortone intently, looking for a sign that would indicate how his approach had been received. But Mortone sat silent and still as a statue. After looking out of the window and watching the boats cruising up and down the river for a moment, Mortone said, "Yes, I agree that I have a need for diversification and also for estate planning. And I probably do spend too much time in this office. But I already have a stockbroker and other advisors. Why would I hand my asset management over to you, Mr. Henderson?"

Tony fingered the report in his hands and thought for a moment before replying. Eventually, he said, "Mr. Mortone, I know I am specially qualified to handle your personal finances. I deal particularly with people like yourself on a regular basis. Unfortunately, I'm not able to reveal her name, but two months ago I took over several million dollars worth of assets belonging to the owner of a local business. She, like yourself, is in her early sixties. Her family is working in the business and will one day assume control over the daily operations. But, for today, she spends her every waking minute in her office keeping the place going. She doesn't have the time for her personal finances either. But together we were able to make solid plans for her retirement. We found substantial tax savings by altering her investment portfolio. And we also managed to convert many of her riskier investments into annuities that will guarantee her income after retirement."

There was another long silence after Tony finished talking as Mr. Mortone considered what he had heard. After a while, he leaned forward, extended his hand with the palm open and said, "Very interesting, Mr. Henderson, please, may I see your plan."

Understanding Mortone's financial risk/return relationships

Even before meeting Mr. Mortone, Tony understood his risk/return relationships because he was familiar with the personal needs and business issues of people who were in the same market. In particular, he knew Mr. Mortone had the same personal needs and business issues as Ivan Kapeck. Mortone was on the verge of retirement and as a result was in the third phase of the financial management cycle — asset management and utilization. He also knew that Mortone was too busy to pay proper attention to his personal finances. As a result, Tony had a clear understanding of Mortone's risk/return relationships. But simply understanding your clients' risk/return relationships is not enough; you must be able to demonstrate your understanding, which takes us to the last strategy — prepare, practice and perfect risk/return scripts.

Strategy 4: Prepare, practice and perfect risk/return scripts

A risk/return script is your guide to how you will show your client you understand them. Your script includes the phrases and stories you will use to reveal the risks faced by your prospects and clients. Because people in the same group have the same risk/return relationships, you can use the same script for all your appointments with people that fall within a single target market. This gives you the opportunity to prepare, practice and perfect your scripts. There is no need to start each appointment from scratch.

Preparing

When you prepare a script you are writing the dialogue long before it will be spoken. In a sense you are playing the role of the playwright. In the quiet of your office or at home in your study, you can take the time to think deeply about the exact words, phrases and stories that will show your clients you understand them. Effective scripts include stories about how you worked with someone to find the solution to a difficult problem. The person in your story should be someone your clients can identify with. They must be able to see that they have the same problem, and your story should motivate them to solve that problem just like the 'hero' or 'heroine' of your story. Even before he met with Mr. Mortone, Tony knew he would be telling him the story of the female entrepreneur — it was something he had prepared long before.

Practicing

When you practice your script, you are changing your role from playwright to actor. As an actor, you read and reread your script. But you are doing more than just memorizing your lines, you are memorizing your delivery, the tone and tempo, the specific emphasis on key words. And like all good actors you must make sure that every time you say your lines you sound natural and sincere. You must also be flexible enough to listen to your client and respond to their concerns, rather than just follow your script blindly.

Perfecting

Perfecting your script means working and reworking your script over time. You will have noticed that Tony said many of the same things to Mr. Mortone as he said to Mr. Kapeck. However, he also introduced new elements, such as his story of the businesswoman. Each time you deliver your lines, study how your prospects and clients respond. Discard the elements that don't work, keep using the elements that prove effective, and always be thinking of new phrases and stories.

The advantages of risk/return scripts

When you use risk/return scripts, you demonstrate your competence and establish your client's confidence in you — both of which are major ingredients in making a sale. We will be taking a closer look at establishing confidence in chapter 6. Another advantage to risk/return scripts is that by using them you will help your clients understand their risks. And because risk motivates people, they will be encouraged to buy your solution to their problem. We'll be exploring risk as motivator more closely in the next chapter.

Best Practice Number 2: Know your client

1) Understand your clients' personal needs.
2) Understand your clients' business issues.
3) Understand your clients' financial risk/return relationships.
4) Prepare, practice and perfect risk/return scripts.

"Hmm," he finally said, "interesting. You've appealed to my sense of the dramatic, my fascination with eternity. It must be my old theater background that makes me a sucker for this, but, tell me more about this $10-million policy."

Chapter 5

Best Practice Number 3: Understand how people make decisions

The first two best practices — develop and utilize a marketing plan, and know your client — will help you create the opportunities you need in order to become a high-performing salesperson. But whether or not you capitalize on those opportunities depends largely on the next two best practices — understand how people make decisions, and help your prospects and clients buy. In this chapter we'll be exploring how people make decisions; in the next chapter we'll be looking specifically at how you can help someone make the right decision — the decision to buy your solution to their problems.

The hidden truths

The third best practice — understand how people make decisions — stands out from the other eight because, although not a single high-performing salesperson lacks it, many don't even know they do it. For example, Kyle, a millionaire salesman, insists he is so successful because he is able to present solutions that are impeccably logical. This ability is certainly an asset, but it is not why he is so successful. His clients do not decide to buy from him because they are impressed with his logical solutions — they buy from him because he understands their values, and because they have confidence in him. Kyle instinctively understands the three most crucial realities about all decisions: 1) all decisions are value based. 2) all decisions are confidence based. 3) all decisions are risk based. In this chapter, we'll be exploring these three truths about decision making so that we can gain the understanding that Kyle naturally possesses.

Decision making truth number 1:
All decisions are value based

In the previous chapter on the second best practice — know your client — we talked about needs and how important it is to know what your client's needs are. Many sales professionals think that people will buy something if they need it — so long as they can afford it. Unfortunately this isn't true. Even when people clearly have the money, they don't always buy the things they need. If your sales technique focuses only on your prospects' or your clients' needs, you will lose many cases you could have won. So, if needs aren't all there is, what else does the salesperson have to know? The answer to this question lies in understanding all the things that motivate someone to make a decision. Let's take a look at what these motivators are.

What motivates people to make a decision

If someone feels they need something, they will be motivated to buy it. But they won't buy it unless they also want it. And more than that, they won't buy it, unless what they need and want is consistent with their values. In fact, these are the three motivators: needs, wants, values. The most crucial motivator is values because they determine whether someone will buy whatever it is they need and want. To put it simply, someone will not buy something, no matter how much they need it, or want it, if they don't feel it fits with their values. To make the interplay between needs, wants and values easy to understand, let me give you an everyday example.

The cheeseburger incident

A couple of weeks ago I met Edward, a client of mine, for a late morning meeting which ran until a little after noon. As I was leaving his office, Edward said, "I've got a big case to work on, but I haven't eaten all day. I need some food. Do you want to grab some lunch?" I had a couple of hours until my next appointment, so I said sure.

We took the elevator down to the main floor and went for a walk along the street, to look for a place to eat. At the corner of the block, we came to a burger joint, its front door wide open. Suddenly my nostrils were filled with the smell of charbroiled hamburgers, and greasy french fries. My mouth watered. Beside me, Edward stopped in his tracks. He was equally overcome. "You know what I want," he turned to me, "a big, juicy cheeseburger — everything on it." His eyes widened.

"I'm game," I said. I had worked out earlier in the morning and felt I had earned a lunch like this. I headed for the open door.

"Norm," Edward called from behind, "I can't."

I looked back at him, his head shaking.

"I want it so bad, but I just can't."

I walked back to the corner. "How come?" I asked.

"I'm watching what I eat now. I haven't had a greasy lunch in months. . . . my health is very important to me."

We ended up at an expensive sandwich bar a couple of blocks away. I had a club sandwich, Edward, a large, healthy gourmet salad — no dressing.

The interplay between needs, wants and values

This story clearly illustrates how the three motivators — needs, wants, and values — determined Edward's decision. There was no doubt he needed food; he hadn't eaten all day, it was lunch time and he was hungry. When it came to the question of what to eat, Edward had a strong desire for a greasy, fattening cheeseburger. But he ended up with a salad instead. And the reason was — although he needed food and wanted the cheeseburger — the cheeseburger was not consistent with the value he placed on his health.

Let's further explore the meaning of Edward's needs, wants and values, by imagining a couple of scenarios.

Imagine that I was in the business of selling food and Edward was one of my customers. If my sales approach was based solely on appealing to his needs and wants, I would have tried to sell Edward a cheeseburger. I would have told him that it was delicious and would satisfy his hunger, but I would not have been able to close the sale. In order to sell anything to Edward, I would have had to have known his values. And, if I had known them, I would have offered him a salad and kept him as a customer.

Now, imagine that the story of our lunch together had turned out differently. Imagine that Edward hadn't called me back from the burger joint. Instead, let's say that Edward had stood there for a few minutes, wrestling with his desire for the cheeseburger, and after a while, despite a valiant effort to exert his will, he had caved in and shuffled shamefully after me into the burger joint. What would this have told us about Edward? Can we say that Edward didn't value his health? Not quite. Clearly Edward was concerned enough about his health to ponder over his decision for a while. What we can say, however, was that the value he placed on his health was not strong enough to overcome his desire. We could also say that this action shows that Edward places a value on enjoying his food and enjoying the moment, and that these values were in conflict with his health value. This story illustrates an important point. It is not enough to know that someone has a specific need, want, and value. We have to know how strong each of them is, and how they conflict with their whole collection of other needs, wants and values.

Let's take a look at how we can better understand someone's particular needs, wants and values.

Values: how we spend our time and money

We can learn a great deal about people, simply by watching how they spend their time and money. Take Edward as an example. He chose to take time out of his day to go somewhere to eat. He could have spent that time any number of ways. He could have forgone any food at all and worked through the lunch hour on his big case, which was important to him. Or, if all he wanted to do was to satisfy his hunger, he could have run downstairs for a quick take-out sandwich and eaten while he worked. How Edward spent his time was an expression of his values. He values his work, but he also strongly values taking the time to relax and eat properly. How Edward spent his money is also an indicator of his values. We didn't have to go to an expensive sandwich bar to eat a healthy meal. Edward could have easily found a salad somewhere nearby for less than the $7.50 he spent.

Time and money are among the most important things we possess, and how we spend them is a clear expression of our values. You can learn a lot about a person by simply watching how they spend their time and money. Let me relate a good example. I first met Steven, a young insurance agent, over a year ago. For the past couple of years he had made $40,000, which he thought was okay for him, considering he had come from a family that never had a lot of money. However, he was complaining about some debt problems and was hoping to find a way to increase his income quickly. When it came time to schedule another meeting he explained to me that he was going to be away on a skiing trip for the next two weeks and would be unable to meet. That told me a lot about his commitment to realizing his potential. He couldn't have been too concerned about money if he was going on an expensive vacation rather than saving his money and working on improving his career. After the meeting ended, Steven offered me a drive downtown. I accepted. In the parking garage, Steven walked up to a new, black Corvette, and opened the passenger door for me. Steven obviously placed so high a value on luxuries like a ski vacation and a fancy car, that he would rather spend his money and credit on them rather than take care of his debts.

Watching people spend their time and money is the best way to understand their values, but not the only way. Through questioning and listening strategies you can uncover someone's needs, wants and values. Knowing how to do this is crucial to helping people buy, because you don't often get to follow your prospects and clients around and study their behavior. You have to be able to figure them out in the short time available in your meeting. We'll be taking a look at these questioning and listening strategies in the next chapter.

I'd like to continue our exploration of needs, wants and values, and how they relate to decision making, by turning to a challenging case one of my clients, Rebecca, experienced.

Rebecca and the sure thing

Rebecca pulled into one of the vacant guest parking spots, tucked behind the corner of a seven-story suburban office building. She glanced down at the digital clock readout: 3:43. She was early. She turned off the engine and the car hummed to a silence. She craned her neck forward and gazed through the windshield at the solid flank of polished glass in front of her. A shudder ran through her. On the top floor was Lincoln Kirkpatrick's office. It was his building — one of his many buildings. And it was state-of-the-art — fully equipped with talking elevators, automatic lighting, and a high-tech security system. Kirkpatrick was a wealthy developer, and the hottest prospect of Rebecca's 6-year career as a life insurance agent.

She had managed to get an appointment with Kirkpatrick through her cousin, Claudia, an architect who had worked on Kirkpatrick's latest project: a movie theater complex. Claudia had gotten along with Kirkpatrick well, and in a discussion at a lunch meeting she bragged to him about her cousin Rebecca and the brilliant insurance packages she puts together. Kirkpatrick admitted he owned no insurance that he knew of, and, at Claudia's behest, agreed to an appointment with Rebecca.

Rebecca sat in the car waiting out the last few minutes, thinking about the case. From what Claudia had told Rebecca, Kirkpatrick was a shrewd, but kind guy, with some very strange ideas and a bizarre sense of humor. He was married and had three young kids he doted on. He worked hard, but always found time to be with his family. Rebecca was amazed to hear that he didn't have any insurance. She knew that few cases were simple, especially when a wealthy business owner was involved, but she had trouble believing that any man would refuse to buy insurance if he loved his family as much as Kirkpatrick did.

When it was a couple minutes before 4:00, she got out of her car, walked around to the front and entered the building. She rode the elevator alone. Rebecca was feeling nervous, but she remembered something I had told her — anxiety is really blocked excitement. As she thought about that, she starting focusing on the exciting opportunity that lay before, and her nervous energy began to dissipate. "Seventh floor, Kirkpatrick Enterprises," the elevator chimed.

Rebecca took a couple of deep breaths before opening the pebbled glass doors to Kirkpatrick's expansive office. She was a little intimidated, but felt confident nonetheless. Kirkpatrick was a loving, family man with loads of money — a perfect candidate for life insurance.

She informed the receptionist that she was there to see Mr. Kirkpatrick, and was promptly ushered down a hallway lined with original art, and into Kirkpatrick's private office. Kirkpatrick, slim and dressed in a collarless leisure shirt, hopped up from his high-backed, studded leather chair.

"Lincoln Kirkpatrick," he introduced himself.

"Rebecca Hoyle."

Kirkpatrick had a full but somewhat unkempt beard, and crazy, Mozart-style hair. His eyes were deep brown, and very young-looking. In fact, he looked like a boy rather than a man. Rebecca instantly felt at ease in his presence.

"Claudia speaks very highly of you, Rebecca. Says you're a wizard with insurance."

"Thank you , Mr. Kirk—"

"Lincoln, please," he interrupted. He motioned for Rebecca to take a seat in one of the chairs opposite his desk, while he resumed his seat in his high-backed chair.

"Lincoln," she began, but was again interrupted.

"Now, I don't know a damn thing about insurance. I'm as healthy as a boy, and fairly well-heeled, Rebecca, so why would someone like me need insurance?"

"Well," Rebecca began, feeling a little less at ease now with the direct challenge, "to protect your kids." From what she had learned from Claudia, his kids were Kirkpatrick's soft spot. Her plan was to zero in on the kids as the reason for the insurance. Kirkpatrick would surely respond to that.

"From what?" Kirkpatrick asked, with a slight smile, as though he was having fun. Rebecca's confidence began to slip. Kirkpatrick was the type of rich man who enjoyed playing people the way a cat plays with mice.

"Well, from your death," Rebecca replied.

"So what if I die?"

"Well—" Rebecca stuttered.

"Well, I'm dead then, aren't I? No more Lincoln Kirkpatrick. May he rest in peace." Kirkpatrick began waving his arms dramatically.

"I, uh—" Rebecca floundered for a reply.

"You plan on bringing me back from the dead, Rebecca?"

"No," she answered, frustrated. She half felt like leaving, but knew to hold her ground. Kirkpatrick was probably just testing her.

"When I die that will be a terrible thing, Rebecca, I assure you, but I don't see what you can do about it," Kirkpatrick said, a little more soberly.

"If you die, Lincoln," she began, "the insurance you have will help provide for your family."

"If it's money your talking about, Rebecca, my kids will be fine."

"But how do you know that, Lincoln?" Rebecca asked.

"My kids will be well taken care of, Rebecca. And their kids will be fine, too. In fact, my kids' kids' kids will be well taken care of. I've built Kirkpatrick Enterprises from scratch. It's a multi-million dollar company now, and growing. Growing fast.

"Right now we're expanding at an incredible pace all along the Pacific Rim. I'm talking about a string of theaters — omniplexes with 3-D, stereo surround sound, giant curved screens 10 stories high, reclining and swiveling plush seats, restaurants instead of snack bars. They'll be springing up all over Taiwan, India, Hong Kong, Singapore, Malaysia, China and Japan in the next two years. That's where the money is. My company will be bulletproof. It'll last forever and when I die it will be my legacy to my children. You see, Rebecca, I have built a money machine, and this machine will print money long after I'm dead. My kids will have nothing to worry about."

"But, Lincoln," Rebecca said, then paused. She was stymied, desperately looking for a reply. She couldn't think of one. She needed to find a hole in his reasoning.

"Yes?" Kirkpatrick asked coyly.

"But the insurance, it's so cheap. For pennies you can buy dollars." She was grasping at straws and she knew it.

"Rebecca, I'm sorry, but I just don't need any insurance. You shouldn't waste your time with me. You should be looking for people who really need it, people who don't have the kind of assets I have." Kirkpatrick rose from his chair and padded out to the center of the room. Rebecca swiveled her chair to face him. He stood there, short, slim shouldered, with his crazy beard and hair, and continued his speech. "Why would I waste any money on insurance premiums, no matter how cheap, when I could put those dollars to work for me in my business. It's my business that's going to provide for my family. And so I have to grow the business as fast as I can. I need every dollar I can get my hands on to keep up with Raji Muhindar, my chief of

Asian expansion, who's out there racing from one end of the continent to the other as we speak. I'll be set for life from the revenues he's generating in India right now. That's by far my biggest market."

Lincoln stopped for a breath and then looked down at Rebecca, "Truth is, I don't take much out of the company. It all goes back into the money machine. You see, someday, when my kids grow up they're going to take over. My daughter, Ruth, she's only 12, but I think she's the one who's going to run this thing. Kirkpatrick Enterprises will be around for a long, long time. That's what keeps me going. It's my dream to build a company that outlives me. Like Disney, Metro-Goldwyn-Mayer, Warner Brothers. That's immortality, Rebecca, that's what I want."

At last, Kirkpatrick finished his sermon. Rebecca was speechless. Kirkpatrick began moving toward the doors to his office, as though to usher Rebecca out. She rose from her chair, and followed him, slowly, shaking her head slightly. She had arrived feeling confident that she could appeal to Kirkpatrick's love for his family, but now that confidence was gone, all gone. It was over. Whatever chance she had, she had lost it. A sense of despair filled her.

"Rebecca," Kirkpatrick said, sticking out his hand, "it was wonderful to meet you. I wish you well."

She was about to extend her hand, but something suddenly stopped her — a vague sensation at the back of her mind. Something inside her was telling her that the case was not over. She wasn't sure how she knew it, but she knew there was still hope. Rebecca stalled by the door while she racked her brains for the answer.

She had come to the meeting confident that she knew how to get Kirkpatrick to make the decision to buy insurance. She knew that Kirkpatrick needed, wanted, and placed a considerable value on protecting his kids. He certainly cared about his kids, and felt he had taken care of their future. Unfortunately Rebecca had failed to show him how insurance could help protect his kids more than he already had. It was beginning to dawn on her — she had made a serious mistake. She had misunderstood what Kirkpatrick's priorities were. She had assumed she knew what Kirkpatrick's current needs, wants, and values were. Unfortunately, protecting his family was not what motivated Kirkpatrick anymore. He was now motivated by another set of needs, wants, and values, and Rebecca had failed to appeal to those. She knew that, as a financial planner, it was her job to help her clients meet their priorities.

Rebecca stood and looked Lincoln Kirkpatrick in the eyes. She was going to give it one more shot. This case was not over, and she knew it. "Lincoln," she said, "let me ask you one more question, if I may."

"Sure," he shrugged.

"What would happen tomorrow morning here at Kirkpatrick Enterprises if you didn't come in?" she asked.

"What do you mean?" he wanted to know.

Rebecca walked back into his office and leaned on the back of the chair. "Let's say that tonight something horrible happens and you die — maybe a freak car accident, doesn't matter. This is hypothetical."

"Oh, there's a happy thought, Rebecca!" Lincoln exclaimed, as he returned to his seat behind his desk. Rebecca also sat down again, and watched Kirkpatrick as he thought about her question, obviously playing out the scenario in his mind. Finally, he said, "I really don't think that much would be different tomorrow. The vice-presidents would step in and run their own departments, they know what they're doing. The board would choose a new CEO. We've got lots of assets, and not all of them are leveraged. In fact, some of our property has doubled or tripled in value since we acquired it. That's a lot of equity." He placed his arms behind his head and smiled at her.

"Well, that's fine," Rebecca said. "You have good employees, I'm sure, and they must be more than capable of running the company without a baby-sitter or you wouldn't have hired them. But, don't forget, you are Lincoln Kirkpatrick — the man behind the name of this company. It is your reputation, your relationships in the industry and your vision which grew this company up from nothing to where it is today. And it is your dream of the future that they are building over in Asia right now. That's what I think the banks are responding to when they lend Kirkpatrick Enterprises money. They lend it to you, not your company. When other companies enter into deals with you, they are dealing with the reputation and genius of Lincoln Kirkpatrick, not some shell run by an unknown vice-president."

Rebecca paused for a second to let that sink in, then said, "However, having said that, let's assume that you're right, and that your company could get along without you."

"Well," Kirkpatrick began, almost in a stutter, "there would be some turbulence, I suppose." Then he flashed a smug smile, "I guess it was my genius that built all this."

Rebecca laughed, then said, "Okay, so, let's look at that another way. You've already told me about your vision of the massive opportunities in the Far East and that, right now, you're really pursuing them aggressively. I'm sure that's an expensive endeavor, so how have you financed those deals?"

"We've leveraged a lot of our property over here to take advantage of the chance to expand over there," Lincoln said. "That's part of the plan."

"Right," replied Rebecca, warming up to the argument. "You've said your company would be okay tomorrow if you died tonight, but what would happen if you died in five years — and in five years the market isn't strong like it is today? Say there's a downturn in the real estate market?

"If you die at the wrong time in the business cycle, your creditors would start to get nervous and begin calling in their loans. They'd want to secure their investments and Kirkpatrick Enterprises would have to start selling assets to meet its obligations. Once that starts happening, it's like dominoes. Your empire could crumble. The money for expansion would dry up, the domestic market would be less profitable because of the downturn and many of your buildings would be gone. It would wipe you out and take Kirkpatrick Enterprises down as well. There would no longer be a Kirkpatrick Enterprises."

Lincoln shifted in his seat. The grimace on his face looked like he had eaten bad seafood. "I never thought of it that way before," he said.

Rebecca moved to the final phase of her argument. If she could show Lincoln a plausible solution that appealed to his needs, wants and values as she had just described them, she was likely to make the sale.

"It doesn't have to be that way," she said. "We can easily protect Kirkpatrick Enterprises from your death."

Lincoln leaned forward in his leather chair.

"On your death we can arrange for a massive infusion of cash into the company coffers to appease the creditors and to help the company survive the transition period until it found new management," she explained.

Lincoln closed his eyes for a second and then leaned back in his chair and said, "So you're asking me to spend money on insurance?"

Rebecca nodded and met his gaze. She didn't let her nerves show. This was a critical junction in the sale.

"Why would I spend the company's money on insurance when I'm using every dollar I can get right now to take advantage of opportunities in the Far East," he asked. A shock ran through Rebecca. That was a logical objection. She needed to find a counterpoint quickly before she lost him for good.

"Let's say, for sake of argument, we take a fraction of your company's worth — $10 million — and then take a fraction of that amount, say $30,000. That's roughly what it would cost as an annual fee to guarantee that on your death $10 million comes into the company. If you don't die, then you can look at it as a waste of $30,000 — I agree. It only works if you die. But if you do die, that $30,000 could save your company from ruin. If you don't pay that $30,000 a year, you could lose your multi-million dollar empire. What would you rather risk losing — $30,000 a year? Or Kirkpatrick Enterprises forever?"

That was the crux of Rebecca's argument. The success of this meeting now hinged on Lincoln's reaction. He made her wait. In silence, he considered the problem while he twisted the chair to the left and right underneath him — dissipating his nervous energy.

"Hmm," he finally said, "interesting. You've appealed to my sense of the dramatic, my fascination with eternity. It must be my old theater background that makes me a sucker for this, but, tell me more about this $10-million policy."

At that moment Rebecca knew she had changed his mind and won the case. Over the next hour they discussed her plan in more detail, arguing out the finer points of the policy and how it would be structured. But he had already made the decision to buy and eventually he agreed to the insurance in the form of a substitute creditor policy.

Priorities: competing needs, wants and values

Although Rebecca had made a mistake in presuming what Kirkpatrick's needs, wants and values were before their meeting, she recovered nicely and won the day. Initially, she had thought he would respond to the value of insurance to his family. However, during the meeting she realized he believed he had already taken care of his kids. His main priority now was building his empire. As a result, Rebecca knew she had to change her approach and appeal to his current needs, wants, and values. She did this by showing him that there were weaknesses in his empire. When Kirkpatrick understood that he was not meeting his priorities, he became interested in what Rebecca could offer him.

Rebecca's experience with Kirkpatrick taught her the importance of needs, wants and values in making a sale, but also that clients may have competing needs, wants and values. She learned that it is imperative to understand the client's priorities and which particular needs, wants and values will motivate the client to make a decision.

I'd like to turn now to the second truth of decision making.

Decision making truth number 2:
All decisions are confidence based

All decisions are confidence based. What this means is that people will decide to do something you recommend only when they have confidence in you. Even if your recommendation is perfectly logical and it is obvious to everyone that you are right, your prospect or client will not decide in favor of your recommendation if they lack confidence in you. As a salesperson, you must understand this crucial truth about how people make decisions, and you must earn the confidence of your prospects and clients.

Let's return to Alvin, the stressed-out, always-late agent, we met in chapter 2.

Alvin: confidence man

There was nothing wrong with Alvin's ability to develop and present solutions. In fact, in this area, he performed very well. He was smart, and had a knack for communicating difficult concepts in simple, easy-to-understand language. Furthermore, he was quite astute at being able to determine and analyze people's needs, wants and values. In fact, it was these abilities that took him to the position of top salesman in the branch. Unfortunately, as we saw in chapter 2, Alvin soon slipped from this position and began languishing in a slump he couldn't get out of. The reason for the slump was that Alvin's prospects and clients lost confidence in him.

Although he didn't know it, Alvin did a number of things that are guaranteed to erode the confidence others have in you. In fact, he did four things in particular that were harmful to how others felt about him: 1) he was always late; 2) he never did what he said he was going to do; 3) he never finished what he started; and 4) he didn't show his appreciation of others. What he was doing was breaking a cardinal set of principles, one that I first heard espoused by a well-known insurance agent, and author of *Breakthrough*, David Cowper. In David Cowper's words, those four principles are:

1) **Be on time.**
2) **Do what you say you're going to do.**
3) **Finish what you start.**
4) **Say please and thank you.**

Because Alvin did none of these things, his prospects and clients had no confidence in him. In chapter 2, I told you about the Doherty case — the big one that Alvin blew. He lost it because he failed to earn Doherty's confidence. During one of our other meetings, Alvin explained to me that in his last conversation with Doherty, Doherty admitted that the proposal Alvin had drawn up had considerable merit. When Alvin had asked why he wasn't going to go ahead with the proposal, Doherty said that he thought it was too good. He felt Alvin had left something out. The truth is Alvin had left nothing out. The proposal was solid, airtight. But because Alvin had been late for his appointments and had handed in the proposal late, Doherty was left with the impression that Alvin was unreliable. If Alvin was unreliable, how could he trust his proposal?

When Alvin realized his problem, he became determined to change his behavior. He began to adopt David Cowper's four principles. He stopped being late, he began to do what he said he was going to do, he started finishing what he started, and he began to take the time to acknowledge people by saying please and thank you. By doing all these things, he began to earn the confidence of his prospects and clients. Instead of losing cases he should have won, he was winning cases he otherwise would have lost. It wasn't long before Alvin resumed his position as top salesperson in the branch.

Decision making truth number 3:
All decisions are risk based

All decisions are risk based. This is true because people are risk averse. People make decisions based on avoiding risk in their lives. If they believe that making a certain financial investment will increase their risk, they will not do it. People always decide to avoid a loss, before they make the decision to pursue a gain. Salespeople who focus only on the gain their clients will make from certain investments, misunderstand the third truth about decision making. By comparison, because high-performing salespeople understand that decisions are risk based, they prefer to expose a loss first, then highlight a gain.

When I explained this third truth to a client recently, they challenged me by saying that they had a friend who decided to purchase a large amount of shares in a mining venture. In fact, their friend used up all of the family savings and put a second mortgage on their home in order to finance the shares. In the end, they had $80,000 worth of stock in just one company, representing nearly their entire investment plan. His friend, however, wasn't worried; he was certain it was a sure thing. Unfortunately, shortly after making the investment the stock collapsed. His $80,000 investment turned into $12 virtually overnight. "How do you explain his decision to buy, if all decisions are risk based?" my client asked.

"Simple," I said. "You've already revealed the answer. You said he was certain it was a sure thing. Although he obviously turned out to be wrong, he didn't see the investment as risky. Rather, he saw not making the investment as a risk, because he didn't want to lose the opportunity to make a killing. His motivation to buy the stocks was based on his attempt to avoid the risk of regretting not buying the stock."

The above story illustrates that wise decisions are made only when people understand the real risks. Investing $80,000 in a single stock when it is nearly everything you have is obviously unwise. But the opposite can also be true. I have an uncle who was raised during the Depression. As a result, he is extremely cautious with his money. For years, he put his entire savings into guaranteed investments, avoiding equities like the plague. Recently, I spent some time with him and his financial advisor, exploring his investment strategy. Obviously he was being too careful. When we showed him that by investing in these low-return deposits, he was actually losing money, once inflation was factored in, he was distressed. He certainly didn't want to be losing money. After we showed him the merits of a more diversified portfolio, he was able to see that a well-managed investment strategy that included equities was not all that risky, and would allow him to grow his money, rather than erode it. Because my uncle wisely saw the risk in being too conservative, he changed his investment strategy. Today, a portion of his money is invested in reliable, blue-chip stocks that will likely return twice as much as his guaranteed investments used to.

If you can understand the three truths we have explored in this chapter — that all decisions are value based, confidence based, and risk based — you will have gained an understanding of how people make decisions, something that is vital to any career in sales. In the next chapter, we'll be looking at how to help people make the decision you want, the decision to buy.

Best Practice Number 3: Understand how people make decisions

1) all decisions are value based.
2) all decisions are confidence based.
3) all decisions are risk based.

People hate to be sold,
but love to buy.

Chapter 6

Best Practice Number 4: Help your prospects and clients buy

When you apply the first three best practices, you are positioning yourself to make a sale, but whether or not you can actually close the deal depends on your ability to apply the fourth best practice — help your prospects and clients buy. It is important to remember that this best practice is not called 'How to sell.' The reason for this is that high-performing salespeople understand that people hate to be sold, but love to buy. So, instead of trying to sell something to their prospects and clients, they help them make the decision to buy.

In this chapter we'll explore the following five strategies involved in helping someone buy: 1) Establish confidence. 2) Identify your prospect's needs, wants and values. 3) Develop the solution. 4) Present the solution. 5) Close. And to illustrate each of these strategies, I'd like to return to Alvin and an important case he worked on.

Strategy 1: Establish confidence

A few months after Alvin and I began working together, he managed to arrange a coveted appointment with Gary Inwood, co-owner of CDD Software.

CDD was a small start-up company, but had recently begun to see some explosive growth. Alvin had read about Gary and his partner, Colin, a number of times in the paper. He had seen many pictures of Gary, a young, intelligent-looking executive, but had never seen a picture of his mysterious, genius partner, Colin. He knew that whoever gained them as a client would have a bright future. CDD was a dream client. Their furious rate of growth would mean constant business. And they were so new, they were sure to have a number of needs that were currently unmet. Even so, they would be a tough client to get, simply because they were so busy and preoccupied with their day-to-day business. Trying to get them thinking about their insurance needs wouldn't be easy, but Alvin was eager to give it a shot. All he had needed was a way to meet Gary, the Chief Operating Officer.

Alvin already had a handful of clients in the software business and had begun calling around to see if any of them knew Gary. Fortunately, Lionel Kent, one of Alvin's long-standing clients, did. He and Gary had been high-school chums. Alvin had asked Lionel if he would introduce him to Gary. "Listen, Alvin," Lionel had said, "if you want an appointment with Gary, call him up and say I sent you. You'll get an appointment if you use my name. He's a good friend, but you do good work, Alvin. I know you won't embarrass me and I'm pretty sure he needs someone to take a look at his insurance." When Alvin put his call in to Gary, he mentioned Lionel's name and that was that. He had his first appointment with Gary the following week.

Alvin realized that the appointment with Gary would be a significant turning point in his career. He had always wanted to find a client who was on the verge of huge success. He had known of other, older agents who made careers out of growing with their clients' rapidly expanding companies. He was eager to take the first crucial steps toward a sale to Gary. And to do that, he knew he needed to use the full power of the fourth best practice.

The appointment was scheduled for one o'clock on Wednesday. At around noon that day, Alvin left his office to head over to meet Gary. CDD was only half an hour away, but Alvin was not going to be late, and he had a couple of quick, but important things to do beforehand anyway. On the way to the elevator, Alvin stopped off in the men's room. He looked at himself in the mirror. His shirt was clean, jacket pressed. He looked professional. He tightened his tie, then left. Down in the concourse area below his building, he found a shoe shine stand and got his wing-tips polished. As he walked to his car in the underground parking, Alvin knew he had taken the first few crucial steps toward making the sale to Gary. Despite what some people might like to think,

Alvin was aware that appearances count. In business, people have more confidence in someone who takes care of themselves. A frayed collar, unpolished shoes — Alvin knew these images would not instill confidence in his prospects.

T minus 3 minutes

Thirty minutes later Alvin pulled his sedan into the small parking area behind the renovated warehouse where CDD had their offices. Inside the small foyer on the main floor, Alvin glanced at the directory. Listed were a couple of dozen companies. By the names, Alvin could tell that nearly all of them had something to do with computers and software. CDD was on the fourth floor. Alvin took a few deep breaths to relax himself. He was always slightly nervous before meeting a new prospect. He had learned in the Marketing & Sales Effectiveness Program* that when someone meets you for the first time they form long-standing impressions within the first three minutes. These impressions are hard to change. According to that theory, he had until 1:03 to establish his confidence with Gary. Fortunately he had a leg up already, simply because he had Lionel's recommendation. Even before meeting him, Gary had reason to trust Alvin. Nothing like a head start, Alvin thought, as he walked over to where the elevator was, pressed the button and waited. There were only four floors, but the elevator was probably 40 years old. It was one of the building's many industrial-age relics — an ironic contrast to the dozens of high-tech, information-age companies that had offices here.

Suddenly, the front door to the building blew open. A young kid was struggling with his bike, trying to haul it inside. He was swearing in frustration. Alvin stood aside as the young kid wheeled his bike across the foyer in front of the elevator. Actually, as Alvin got a better look, he noticed that the kid wasn't so young. Well, not a teenager at least, probably late 20s. He was tall and skinny, and had scraggly, long black hair, which he kept swishing off his face. He was wearing what looked like a brightly colored bathing suit, sneakers and a Dairy Queen T-shirt.

At last, the elevator arrived, its doors yawned open, slowly, and with a grating whine. The cyclist shoved his bike into the elevator.

*MSEP IS AVAILABLE THROUGH THE COVENANT GROUP

Alvin followed behind, careful not to get grease on his suit. Eventually the doors shut, and the elevator began its grinding ascent.

Inside the cramped elevator, Alvin focused on being relaxed and comfortable, and practiced in his mind how he was going to greet Gary — with a confident smile and a firm handshake. Natural, not affected. Alvin's concentration was broken by his neighbor who had begun grunting and muttering. Alvin was no computer wizard, but it sounded to him like the cyclist was trying to solve, out loud, some nagging computer design issue. He heard words like 'query language,' 'database transaction,' 'authoring system,' 'bits per second.'

At the fourth floor the elevator jolted and came to rest. The doors widened and the eccentric cyclist marched out, dragging his bicycle behind him. Alvin shook his head in amazement. The world was made up of all kinds. He stepped off the elevator and looked around. A placard on the opposite wall indicated that CDD was located to the left.

Alvin turned left and walked down the hall, the cyclist a few yards ahead of him. Halfway down the corridor, the cyclist turned into one of the offices. As Alvin continued, he realized that the cyclist had just entered the offices of CDD. Alvin followed behind him.

In the reception area, Alvin saw the cyclist march past the front desk and disappear behind a corner. I guess he works here, Alvin thought to himself. He wondered what he did.

"Hi, I'm here to see Gary. I'm a little early," Alvin said to the receptionist.

"I'll let him know," she said, then asked, "your name?"

"Alvin Benson."

After waiting a couple of minutes, Alvin was ushered in to see Gary who stood up from behind his desk and came over to say hello. He was wearing a double-breasted blue suit, and a fat, red tie.

Alvin smiled, and reached out his hand.

"Hi, Gary. How are you?" he said in a warm, friendly voice. Alvin was aware that the way he spoke — the tone, the tempo — was critical. He knew that 93% of what you communicate is not what you say, but how you say it, and your body language. Alvin also understood that simply by believing in his own abilities, he would be able to convey, through his body language, a deep, inner confidence and peace.

"Fine. Busy, but fine," Gary replied.

"From what I've read and from what Lionel has told me about CDD, you guys are extremely busy. I think it's amazing how you've managed to make such an impact so quickly," Alvin said, waiting for Gary to offer him a seat.

"Thanks," Gary replied, smiling at the compliment, "the roof's blowing off this place. It's exciting, but we're all going mental with stress. There's no pressure like a software deadline. In this business if you ship late, you can be ruined." Gary pointed toward one of the black leather chairs opposite his desk, and said, "Please, sit down, Alvin."

Alvin sat down, leaned back comfortably in the chair, and breathed slowly and deeply — looking relaxed and confident. He knew not to appear nervous. If you're tense and defensive — fidgeting and breathing shallowly — you'll make your prospect tense and defensive as well. But if you're relaxed, you'll go a long way toward putting your prospect at ease, and creating an environment where they feel free to open up and give you the information you need.

"So, how's Lionel?" Gary asked. "I haven't seen him in a couple of weeks."

"Good. We played some pool the other night. I guess you're aware Lionel's quite the hustler."

"I've heard, but I don't play."

"What do you play?" Alvin asked, hoping he could get a rapport going.

"I'm a golfer."

"Oh, really, where do you play?" he asked Gary.

"Glendan Dale."

"Nice club. I've played there a couple of times with a client of mine who's a member — Yuri Onofsky."

Yuri was another one of Alvin's computer business clients. He was co-owner of a company that set up computer networks for small and medium-sized corporations. In the past few years Yuri's company had tripled in size. Alvin was hoping Gary knew who Yuri was.

"Yuri," Gary said, raising his eyebrows. "You know Yuri?"

"We've been doing business together for a few years now."

"Yuri's quite a guy," Gary said. "They say he's a genius."

"He's no dummy," Alvin replied wryly.

Gary laughed.

"By the way, do you have a handicap?" Alvin asked.

"Yeah, fifteen. You?" Gary said smiling, obviously proud.

"Twenty. You manage to get out much lately?"

"Not really," Gary replied, sagging. "I think I've only gone three times this year, and the summer's half over. I used to play three times a week. In the good old days before CDD."

Alvin and Gary continued to talk about golf for another couple of minutes. Gary explained how he had been trying a new swing that would certainly change his game — if only he had the time to practice and put it to use. At one point, Gary came around the desk and demonstrated the swing — using a ruler for a golf club.

"I used to bring the club back more like this," Gary said, swinging his arms back in a wide, flat arc. "But now I try to make things more up and down — like this." He brought his arms back more vertically — in a sweeping, pendulum-like motion.

"The difference is incredible," Gary declared.

Gary had clearly warmed up to Alvin, but Alvin still had a couple more things to do in order to further establish his confidence. First, he wanted to let Gary know that he was familiar with the high-tech business. And then, second, he wanted to show Gary that he had his best interests at heart. To do those two things he would need to steer the conversation gently away from the topic of golf, and toward business matters. Fortunately, he had already introduced Yuri into their dialogue.

"The last time I played was with Yuri," Alvin said. "He kicked my butt, to tell the truth. He's pretty close to a scratch player. He tells me he plays pretty regularly. Conducts a lot of business on the golf course. And from the way his company's taken off, the golf strategy seems to be working. Actually, that's when Yuri and I started working together. When his business started to expand like that, he became concerned about the risks he was taking. Another client of mine, Simon Hayword, who owns Hayword Tech, recommended me to

Yuri. Yuri and I ended up putting together a whole plan to help reduce the risk both inside and outside his company."

Alvin spent the next few minutes describing in greater detail how he had helped many of his other high-tech clients manage the financial risks in their personal and business lives.

Now it was time to show that he had Gary's best interests at heart.

"Gary," Alvin began, "when we talked on the phone, I said I wanted to come see you to talk about managing the risk in your business. Perhaps we'll be able to do some of the same things I've done with Yuri and Simon. I do want to make it clear that my purpose in being here is for you to become a client of mine. And one of the things I've learned is that for any client relationship to succeed, you must value what I bring to the relationship. So, let me ask you — what are you looking for in a financial advisor."

Gary leaned back in his chair and stared at the ceiling, thinking. "I guess there are a couple of things that are important to me."

"May I ask what they are?"

"I'm tired of people who promise great service and don't deliver," Gary said, "so that's one of the key things. Excellent service. And then the other thing would be working with someone who really understands my business. A lot of the suppliers and salespeople we get coming through our office don't really have a grasp of our business. . . . But I guess you've got a leg up there, having already worked with high-tech clients."

By now, Alvin felt he had fulfilled the first strategy — he had established confidence. This was a significant feat. Gary was the business brains behind a software company that was riding the crest of a massive tidal wave. They had made several million last year, and, according to the papers, were poised for revenue in the high seven figures. Alvin glanced briefly at a clock on the wall — a few minutes after one o'clock. Right on time, Alvin thought to himself. He experienced a momentary feeling of relief. Things were going smoothly, but he knew he had a long way to go, and he prayed that Gary would hang on for the ride. Anyone as busy as Gary could suddenly decide they had more important things to do than spend time talking to a salesperson. Alvin had to manage this interview carefully.

Confidence

Before continuing with the story, I'd like to briefly discuss the importance of the first strategy and recap how Alvin managed to establish confidence with Gary.

In chapter 5, we saw that all decisions are confidence based — a prospect will not buy from you unless they have confidence in you. Many struggling salespeople forget or neglect to create the necessary confidence. Confidence is something you have to establish as quickly as you can. Remember, the first three minutes of your first appointment are critical — during those three minutes your prospect will form their impressions of you. If they view you as credible and trustworthy, you'll be able to move smoothly through the next four buying strategies. If they have questions about your character and doubt your abilities, you might not even get the opportunity to proceed. When you build your prospect's confidence in you, you are preparing them to make a buying decision. Now, let's quickly review the many ways Alvin executed this first strategy.

Purchasing confidence

Alvin did a number of things that are extremely effective at establishing confidence. The very first thing he did was purchase some immediate confidence by gaining a referral from a friend of his prospect. Because Gary has confidence in his friend, Lionel, he will automatically have confidence in someone Lionel recommends. This is like the saying, 'any friend of yours is a friend of mine.' To further build on the referral and remind Gary of their mutual friend, Alvin made a point of mentioning Lionel's name right at the beginning of the appointment.

Dress

You build confidence by entering your prospect's world. Before the meeting, Alvin did something that was key to establishing his confidence — he made sure he was dressed appropriately for the occasion, and well-groomed. From the articles and pictures of Gary that Alvin had seen, he knew Gary was a businessman who wore a suit and tie to work, and that he would respond positively to someone who dressed similarly. By comparison, Alvin has a number of clients in the graphic design business. When he goes to see them, he dresses neatly, but more casually.

Mannerisms

When Alvin greeted Gary, he did so in a friendly, confident manner, and during the meeting conveyed a credible image in a variety of non-verbal ways — through his tone of voice, slow, even breathing, and relaxed posture. Keep in mind that only 7% of what you say is the words you use — the rest comes through your manner and body language. Through non-verbal means, Alvin was able to communicate a quiet self-confidence.

Rapport

Alvin put Gary at ease by building rapport. He began by complimenting Gary on the success of his business, and did so in a genuine fashion. Nothing is less credible than a smarmy, oily compliment. And by launching a brief discussion about golf, Alvin encouraged Gary to relax and treat him as a trustworthy friend. As a bonus, Alvin and Gary discovered they had another mutual acquaintance — Yuri. Within minutes of meeting Gary, Alvin had moved from being a stranger to being someone with whom Gary shared common ground.

Competence

When Alvin began talking about how he worked with other people in the high-tech industry, he was showing Gary that he understood his problems, that he would be able to help him, because he had helped others like him. In effect, he was showing Gary that he was competent.

Positive intent

The next thing Alvin did was communicate his positive intent. Alvin understood that his growth as a salesperson depended on his ability to help Gary achieve his goals. Alvin showed Gary that his intention was a positive one for both himself and, especially, Gary. He did this by asking Gary what he would be looking for in a financial advisor.

This proved to Gary that he was there not just to make a sale, but to give Gary what he wanted.

Strategy 2: Identify your prospect's needs, wants and values

After establishing confidence, Alvin's next step was to identify Gary's needs, wants, and values. But Alvin knew he couldn't simply jump right in and start grilling him. If he let loose with a barrage of personal questions, Gary would likely clam up, and all the confidence he had established would go to waste. He needed to set the stage for strategy 2, and to do that he had to ask for Gary's permission to proceed; that way Gary would feel he was willingly answering a series of questions that served a purpose, rather than exposing himself for no reason.

"Gary," Alvin began, "in order to see if there is anything we can do together, we'll need to explore your situation in more depth. Would it be all right if I asked you a few questions about your business?"

"Sure," Gary replied, "go ahead."

Earning the right to proceed

With Gary's consent, Alvin had just earned the right to proceed. He knew that it was important to get his prospect's approval along the way. Each approval was like a little close that took him one step closer to a signed application. Without earning the right to proceed at vital moments, you run the risk of losing your prospect, and creating resistance.

Over the next while, Alvin would endeavor to uncover what Gary's needs, wants and values were. And like any good detective, he would do that by asking questions, listening, and observing Gary's body language. He would start with a series of information questions that Gary would find easy to answer, and then move to more probing questions that would explore Gary's feelings.

Information questions: Gary's current situation

In order to identify needs, wants and values, Alvin would first have to establish what Gary's current situation was. This is what the information questions were designed to uncover.

"Gary," Alvin began, "how old is your company?"

"Well, if you go back to the very beginning, it's four years old."

"How did you get started?"

"Four years ago I was working as an accountant in a small firm. I was the youngest guy there, and so I got all the really small clients. Everyone else was working on established, successful accounts. I was paying my dues, and I knew it. Anyway, there was this one crazy guy named Colin Drayton, who walked into our offices looking for an accountant. He looked like a freak. He had long hair, and was dressed like a bum. Somehow he managed to convince the receptionist that he needed an accountant and could afford one. So, she put the call through to me. Reluctantly I went out to greet this guy. Immediately I was trying to think up ways to throw him out, without being obviously rude. But before I could make a move, he started prattling on about this start-up company, and these software products he had designed. And then he mentioned something about a contract for a quarter of a million dollars. I thought he was nuts, but decided to give him the benefit of the doubt." As Gary continued to tell the story, he grew considerably more spirited. He obviously enjoyed recounting the early days. The information Gary was revealing was valuable, and Alvin leaned forward in his chair to show Gary he was interested, and to encourage him to tell the whole story.

"So I invited Colin back to my office, and we talked about his situation for a while. Actually, we spent the rest of the day together. It didn't take me long to realize that this guy was a genius — but a genius in a very specialized area. He knew everything about computers and programming and nothing at all about anything else. I took him on as a client, and we sorted through his books and his financial situation. It was a mess, but he was making money that's for sure. Loads of it. I thought, if he was able to make money being this disorganized, he'd be able to make tons with a plan and some business acumen to back him up. After a few weeks of working together I made a proposal to him. I asked him if he wanted to start a company together with me. I told him, 'Look, you won't ever have to worry about the business side of things again. All you have to do is concentrate on the products.' He went for it. We incorporated a company. He took 50%, and I took 50%. He builds the products, and I make all the financial decisions. I'm as dumb about computers as he is about business. We're a great team."

Alvin was glad to know he was dealing with the decision maker. He knew that Colin would go along with any proposal so long as Gary agreed to it.

"That's a hell of a story," Alvin said. "It's amazing that you were able to spot the potential in Colin, and then begin capitalizing on it so soon."

At that moment someone came barging into the office. Alvin turned his head and noticed it was the cyclist.

"Server's acting up. Damn it. Damn Database — queries aren't getting through," the cyclist said, as he stood in the middle of the room.

Alvin looked at Gary who smiled.

"Meet Colin Drayton — the infamous Colin David Drayton," Gary said to Alvin.

Alvin gulped. This is the genius. The cyclist from the elevator. Alvin masked his surprise, stood up, smiled and reached out his hand toward Colin. His hand hung in midair.

"Colin's not much for social niceties, Alvin," Gary said. "Don't take it personally."

In fact, Colin didn't even acknowledge Alvin's presence. He was still muttering on about his computer problems.

Gary winked at Alvin, then got up from his chair and led Colin out into the hall. They talked there for a few minutes. Alvin could hear Colin swearing, and slapping the wall in anger. A few moments later, Gary returned shaking his head.

"I go through this a few times a day. It's part of my duties — I have to baby-sit him. But hell, if that's what it takes to keep him going, I'm not going to complain."

"If you need any help baby-sitting, just let me know," Alvin said, laughing.

"I'll keep that in mind," Gary replied, smiling, then returned to his seat.

"Colin David Drayton," Alvin repeated aloud, suddenly figuring out the source for the company name. "That's where CDD comes from, I guess."

"Yep," Gary replied, "Colin's got a bit of the ego in him. He didn't want to use any of my initials, which was fine. I don't have any trouble being the man behind the scenes — the money's the same, and that's what matters to me."

Already, even during the information-gathering stage, Gary was beginning to reveal his values. Alvin was excited that Gary had begun to open up so early. But he still needed quite a bit more information.

"Do either of you have families?"

"Me, I'm married. We have a three-year-old boy, Sean. . . . As for Einstein there, well, he's married to his computers. I can't imagine him living with anyone, or anyone living with him." Gary laughed thinking about Colin's social life.

"So, is that still how the ownership stands — split between you two?" Alvin asked. "Or have you sold shares along the way?"

"No, still fifty-fifty."

"And how many people do you employ?"

"We have twelve full-time employees, and a handful of people we call on for part-time or contract work whenever we hit a crunch time."

"Obviously things have been moving very quickly for you, but may I ask whether you've had the chance to put a proper shareholders agreement in place?"

Gary sighed. "There's a few things we haven't really caught up on — and that's one of them. We've been back and forth with the lawyers, but to tell the truth, it gets lost in the shuffle."

"In the proposed agreement, is there a buy-out clause?"

"There will be, when it's done."

"Would the agreement provide for you to buy-out each other's shares?"

"Yes, that's the way we'd want it."

"Can you tell me what the company is worth today?"

"Around $4 million."

"Let me ask you, as well, Gary, whether you have a bank loan, or a line of credit."

"For a long while all we ever had was a line of credit. We were really fortunate in the first couple of years because our cash flow was strong, and we didn't have the overhead we have now. Two of Colin's early products — a software product that analyzes stock portfolios and another that tracks currency movements around the world —

kept us solidly in the black. But we started making some moves to expand pretty aggressively. Last year we went for a business loan. That was when we moved in here and hired half a dozen people. We also shipped six new products in a two-month period."

"What was the loan for?"

"Half a million."

"Is the loan insured?"

"You mean life insurance? No, it's not."

"What about any other insurance, Gary. Are either you or Colin insured?"

"I think I still have an old policy, probably not worth much. I got it when I was with the old firm. As for Colin, I'm pretty sure he doesn't have a thing."

Alvin sensed that Gary had a negative attitude toward insurance. He didn't own much himself, and didn't seem too concerned. He had, however, agreed to meet, which was a positive sign. He obviously trusted Lionel's advice, but Alvin worried about how deep his bias against insurance might run.

Analytical questions: Gary's desired situation

Alvin and Gary continued to talk about the business for a few more minutes. Eventually Alvin felt he had a good grasp of Gary's current situation. Now it was time to further explore Gary's needs, wants and values by trying to understand his desired situation. To do that, he would have to change his questioning tactic. Instead of information questions, he would have to ask analytical ones, questions that would not only help him understand Gary, but would also help Gary understand himself. In all likelihood, Gary had never considered some of these questions. And they would be a little tougher than the information questions, because Gary would have to reflect on the answer before speaking. There was no simple right or wrong response. Alvin crossed his fingers that Gary would co-operate.

"Gary, let me ask you what you think your growth potential is — say over the next five years."

Gary leaned back in his chair, and gazed toward the ceiling. He let out a little gleeful huff. "Huge. In five years we'll be enormous, I know that for sure. When I first started with Colin four years ago, we did a 5-year plan. We've already far exceeded those expectations, but we revise the plan every year, and the latest version shows us being close to the $50-million mark five years from now."

"Have you thought beyond that, Gary?"

"Well, our plan is to go public at that point. Do an offering and then really take this baby to the stars. We're planning an IPO generating $250 million."

As Alvin expected, Gary was very clear about his business goals, but Alvin needed to clarify what his personal goals were.

"And what are *your* plans, Gary?" Alvin asked. "Do you plan to stay with the company? Or sell off some time soon?"

"Nope, I'm sticking with this puppy. You don't get many chances like this, and I'm going to ride this one out — for the next ten years at least. And then I'll probably spend the rest of my life spending all the money I've made."

Gary had clearly expressed what he wanted — to retire in ten years. This was what drove him to work such long hours, under such pressures. Alvin was glad Gary had articulated so clearly his desired goal — it was exactly what Alvin needed to move forward.

Feeling questions: exposing the gap

Alvin and Gary talked a little bit longer about Gary's plans. Alvin had a clear understanding that the company meant everything to Gary, and that Gary was eager to realize all of CDD's potential — in order to achieve his goal of retiring young. Unfortunately, there were a number of significant holes in Gary's current situation, and Alvin wondered whether or not Gary realized just how fragile things were. It was time to grab Gary's attention by pointing out the gap between his current and desired situations. This gap would be Gary's risk/return relationship. As we saw in the last chapter, all decisions are risk based; if Alvin could make Gary understand what his risks were, he would be able to motivate him to reduce those risks. In his book, *Breakthrough*, David Cowper tells us how he uses risk to motivate clients to buy, by applying strategies for finding and exposing what he refers to as 'The Loss.' To begin exposing Gary's risk, Alvin would need to use feeling questions.

Alvin began by giving a brief synopsis of both Gary's current and desired situations. "Gary," he said, "as I understand it, CDD is a company jointly owned by you and Colin. You have employees, but the business is totally dependent on the two of you. Without your combined efforts, skills, and genius, CDD wouldn't exist." Gary nodded. "CDD is experiencing some dramatic growth, and has a lot of potential and the two of you are totally committed to realizing that potential." Again Gary nodded.

"If, for whatever reason, either of you couldn't come in tomorrow, things would be disrupted, I imagine," Alvin said.

"Yes. I suppose you mean what would happen if Colin got hit by a bus?" Gary asked defensively. Alvin watched in horror as Gary leaned back in his chair and folded his arms. Not a very good sign. Alvin's stomach fell. Gary's negative bias to insurance was coming out. Alvin had to figure out a way to disarm Gary, and quickly.

Immediately, Alvin leaned back in his chair, and assumed a very relaxed posture. He didn't want Gary to think he was on the attack. He knew that by positioning himself in an unguarded manner, he would encourage Gary to open up again. As he sat back, he noticed Gary's rigid posture slacken. A wave of relief washed over Alvin. Now he had to reestablish some confidence.

"I've worked on a number of situations similar to CDD. The great thing about a partnership like yours is the incredible potential. You get two people who are so talented in completely different ways and put them together and the result is frequently dynamic. The downside is that the two people are very dependent on each other." Alvin noticed Gary lean forward with more interest now. Alvin moved forward in his seat to mirror him — a way of saying he had Gary's interests at heart. He continued, "You've already said that you know nothing about computers and that Colin's equally at a loss when it comes to business. Imagine having to step in and do Colin's job, for even a week. And imagine what the banks would say when they found out Colin wasn't able to work." Alvin stopped, and let Gary react to what he just said.

"It's a house of cards, eh," Gary sighed.

"Well, it doesn't have to be like that, that's for sure. It's a matter of protecting yourself against contingencies. Right now you have strong, ambitious plans. You want to retire in 10 years time."

Gary nodded.

"Let me ask you how you feel about those dreams being dependent on Colin's ability to come in here everyday in perfect health for the next ten years."

Gary shook his head. "Frankly, I'll probably lose some sleep tonight thinking about it."

"I'd like to ask you one more thing, Gary. How do you plan on financing your buy-out agreement?"

"Through corporate revenues."

"And in the event of Colin's death?"

"Same way, I suppose," Gary replied, then thought about his answer. "But I guess his death would have a significant impact on the company."

"Let me ask the question the other way around. Let's say it's you that dies. I'm sure you'd be a lot more comfortable knowing that you were able to guarantee Colin had the money to purchase those shares from your estate. I'm sure your family would rather not wait while Colin struggled on his own, trying to keep CDD going."

Again Gary nodded in agreement.

Alvin glanced at his watch and noted that their time was just about up. He needed Gary's approval to go away and put a plan together. "Gary," Alvin said, "I can think of a number of ways we can work together to put you at ease. Would you like me to go away and develop a plan that will make you sleep better at night?"

"Yes."

They shook hands, and Alvin left CDD with the go-ahead he was after.

Full sensory communication

This interview Alvin had with Gary is a wonderful example of the second strategy — identifying your prospect's needs, wants, and values. After Alvin earned the necessary right to proceed, he carefully applied an effective questioning approach, beginning with information questions, moving on to analytical questions, and then ultimately to questions designed to expose the 'gap' and sound out Gary's feelings. But Alvin did much more than ask questions. He listened, and listened actively — whenever he asked a question, he studied Gary's reaction, and judged the response. Active listening is critical to an effective interview, because it allows you to detect biases your prospect might have. It is important to be receptive to and understanding of your prospect's bias, especially if it is a bias you do not possess yourself. Alvin knew that someone's bias will affect how they make a decision. It is something you can't ignore. You have to find a way to neutralize the bias. A significant bias arose during Alvin's interview, but he was able to respond properly. At one point — when Gary crossed his arms — Alvin knew that Gary held a bias against insurance. Accordingly, Alvin knew to back down. Had he kept up a more direct, aggressive approach, he would have certainly driven Gary deep into a defensive shell, and the culmination of the meeting would probably not have been a positive one. Alvin also applied effective non-verbal techniques, like body-mirroring, in order to communicate with Gary. As well, Alvin's careful choice of the word 'we' instead of 'I' at the end of the meeting further reinforced that he was working on Gary's behalf, not his own. We'll see how important using 'we' instead of 'I' can be in the next chapter.

Strategy 3: Develop the solution

After you've identified your prospect's needs, wants, and values, you are ready to develop a solution. You must design a solution that bridges the gap between the prospect's current situation and where they want to be — their desired situation. Your solution must meet their needs and wants, and remain in line with their values.

When you develop a solution for your prospect you are essentially clarifying their intention. Alvin knew the power of a clear intention, because it had changed his own life. With a clear goal of becoming a high-performing salesperson, Alvin was becoming more successful each day. Now, through questioning and listening, Alvin was able to help Gary understand his own intentions — what was important to him and what his goals were. It was Alvin's role to develop a solution that would help Gary and Colin realize their dreams.

When Alvin started developing the solution for Gary, he knew Gary's goal was to build CDD to a point where he could leave the company and live off his wealth. But he had made it clear to Gary that the present situation was fragile, that it left the door open for disaster to strike. By the end of the interview, both Alvin and Gary were aware that Gary was unhappy about leaving his dreams of retirement up to chance. Clearly, Gary wanted to protect them from being scuppered as much as possible. As an insurance broker, Alvin would be able to guard against a number of tragic events, such as the death or disability of either Colin or Gary.

After their initial meeting, Alvin spent two weeks developing a comprehensive insurance package that would solve Gary and Colin's problem. When he was finished, he telephoned Gary and set up another appointment.

Strategy 4: Present the solution

At two o'clock on Thursday afternoon, Alvin was led into Gary's office by the receptionist.

Gary sat behind his desk and invited Alvin to sit in the chair across from him.

"Actually, Gary, do you mind if we use your couch over there. I have some things I'd like to spread out on the coffee table."

"Sure," Gary agreed, a little stiffly, getting up from his chair to move over to the couch in the corner.

Alvin was not discouraged by Gary's cool reception. He knew to expect Gary to be more aloof today than during their last meeting. In the days between their meetings, Gary would have been too busy to give the subject of insurance much thought, and by now his defenses would be up again. Alvin knew that it was important to disarm Gary, to reestablish their rapport and ease into the presentation. This was why he didn't want to sit in the chair. Looking at Gary across the expanse of his giant desk would encourage an adversarial tone. It would be too easy for Gary to hide behind his mahogany fortress. But, by sitting beside each other on the couch, Alvin would be able to show Gary that they were a team, working together to solve his problems.

On the couch, Alvin began by restating Gary's problem, just to make sure they both agreed what his needs were. "Let's begin with a review of your situation as I understand it. Last time we met, Gary, we came to the conclusion that your plans to retire from your business in ten years had some obvious vulnerabilities. In particular, we realized that the success of CDD depends on you and Colin being able to come to work everyday for the next 10 years. Were something to happen — an accident, or a death — the company would surely suffer. Loans would be called, and there would likely be a problem financing the purchase of the other guy's shares." Alvin paused and looked at Gary, waiting for a response. Gary nodded, showing Alvin he agreed.

"However," Alvin began again, "we can protect against the problems quite easily. There's no reason why your dreams of retiring young have to be dependent on Colin's health. That is a heavy risk for you to take, but there are others out there who are in the business of taking on those risks, namely the company I represent. Last year alone, Olympus Life insured over 100,000 people."

Gary raised his eyebrows.

"Gary," Alvin said, "I spent a great deal of time last week figuring out the best way to protect your business and your dreams of retiring. I came up with three different packages, all of which offer you the protection you need. I'd like to show them to you now, so we can explore how they'll help you. And you'll be glad to know that we can implement any one of them right away."

Alvin reached into his briefcase, took out a set of proposals and then laid them across the teak coffee table. "Each of these proposals contains an insurance plan that will fund your buy-out, and, at the same time, provide funds for the company to tide it over until a suitable replacement can be found for either you or Colin." Alvin paused, and Gary leaned forward to take a closer look at the plans.

Over the next couple of minutes Gary asked Alvin questions about how the plans worked, what the premiums were and how many years he would have to pay them. Alvin answered each question directly and confidently.

After a while, Gary looked up and said, "I don't know, Alvin. It's just the idea of insurance, I guess. I don't like thinking about death."

Alvin took a deep, slow breath. There was a lot riding on how he responded to Gary's remarks. He wanted the sale more than anything, but being aggressive or sounding desperate would only drive Gary back behind his wall of defenses. He would have to frame his presentation in a way that would show Gary the benefits of the insurance. To do that he would have to demonstrate the consequences of not going with one of the proposals. Gary would have to understand that doing nothing was, in itself, a very big and risky decision. But first, Alvin would have to disarm Gary's negative reaction. "Gary," Alvin began, "no one likes to think about death. We shouldn't be thinking about it that way; we should be thinking about your retirement. That's what these plans are all about. If you don't go ahead with one of these plans, what you are in effect saying is that you would prefer to take on the risk of Colin dying."

Gary put his head in his hands. Alvin knew that the thought of depending on Colin — the irascible, mad genius — was not a pleasant one for Gary. Alvin let Gary think some more, then started in with a quick story. It was time to close.

"Gary," he said, "last year I met with someone who was in a position similar to the one you are in now. This person owned a company jointly with someone else. They ran a small, but very profitable advertising company. The guy I met was the business brains, and the other guy was the creative genius. I pointed out how vulnerable the company was because it was entirely dependent on the two of them being able to work together. A few months later, the guy called me up and told me his partner had just been diagnosed with cancer. He was devastated. They'd been in business together for over 10 years. It was a massive brain tumor, and he died a couple months after that." Alvin stopped talking.

Gary looked up expectantly.

"Their company dissolved. There was no way to continue it without the creativity they were famous for." Alvin paused again briefly. "But fortunately they were both insured. My client was able to close the business down with dignity. He's semi-retired now."

Gary nodded.

Alvin's presentation procedure

Before we move on to see how Alvin finally closed the sale, I'd like to quickly review Alvin's presentation procedure.

Reestablish rapport

The first thing Alvin did was reestablish a rapport with Gary. This step is vital. If you don't do it, you risk dealing with a prospect who will be resistant to your proposals. You must reconnect with your prospect so that they will be open to your ideas.

Review the problem

The next thing Alvin did was review the problem with Gary. Again, this is a crucial step. You must never assume your prospect remembers what his problem is. By restating the problem, you make it top-of-mind again. Plus, it allows you to ensure that your prospect and you agree on what the problem is. Note that after going over the problem, Alvin waited for Gary to nod his assent.

Convert the problem into an opportunity

Right after reviewing the problem, Alvin's next move was to convert the problem into an opportunity. He did this by explaining to Gary that there was something they could do, that Gary did not have to risk his retirement on Colin's health.

Reminder of credentials

Another important thing Alvin did was remind Gary of his credentials. He did this by mentioning the company he represented, and referring to the number of policies it put in force last year. This showed Gary that thousands of other people made the decision to buy, and created a sense of confidence in the proposal Alvin was about to present.

Preview for action

Before proceeding with his presentation, Alvin mentioned that Gary would be able to immediately go ahead with any of the proposals he showed him. This was an effective way of preparing Gary to buy, without putting any pressure on him. When it came time to close, Gary would have already been exposed to the idea of doing something right away.

Frame the presentation

The next key thing Alvin did was frame the presentation in a way that showed Gary the consequences of not buying the insurance. This step is crucial. Too many salespeople focus on the features of the plan. Instead, you must highlight the benefits of your solution to the client. One very effective way of underscoring the benefits is to show them the cost of not making a decision. Insurance is an intangible. It is not something the client can take away with them. That's why so many prospects find it easy to say no to insurance. But once they understand the cost of saying no, they are more likely to say yes. Again, it is important to make your prospect aware that it is impossible for them not to make a decision; simply doing nothing is a decision, and one with heavy consequences. Furthermore, Alvin framed the presentation as a direct solution to Gary's problem.

Make it tangible

The next thing Alvin did was make the insurance solution tangible by telling a story. This made it real to Gary. Insurance was no longer just a piece of paper, it was something that had a serious impact on someone's life.

Use of 'we'

Another important thing Alvin did was continue to use 'we' rather than 'I' throughout the presentation. By doing this he reaffirmed that he and Gary were both on the same side.

Strategy 5: Close

Alvin knew he was ready to close now. It was time to request the action he had set up earlier when he told Gary they would be able to implement one of the proposals right away. Alvin was not nearly as nervous as he used to be when he first started selling insurance. Back then, closing was a big deal. It was a momentous moment. Not that Gary's ultimate decision didn't mean much — it meant everything. But Alvin knew he had prepared Gary for the close. He had, in fact, made little closes along the way. Each time he got Gary's approval or agreement, each time he waited for Gary to nod, he was moving that much closer to the final buying decision. The close now would be a natural step in the evolution of the meeting. Gary was expecting it as much as Alvin was.

Another thing that is important to closing is making sure that you are speaking to the decision maker. The proposal Alvin was asking Gary to decide upon would affect Colin as much as it affected Gary. In this case, Alvin knew that Gary ran the business and made all the financial decisions. So long as Gary supported the insurance proposal, Colin would agree. It was not necessary to involve Colin in the meeting.

Alvin looked at Gary and asked, "Which of these three options do you prefer?" It was an easy question, because it assumed the sale already. Alvin wasn't asking Gary to make an overt commitment; he was implying that Gary was already committed, which was a fair assumption because Gary had agreed to come this far in the meeting.

"Well, I like the third option," Gary said.

Alvin silently breathed a sigh of relief. It was over. He'd made the sale.

"But—" Gary continued.

Alvin felt his heart jolt, and looked at Gary.

"But, I'm not sure I like the premiums. The idea of paying all that money."

How Alvin responded now would mean the difference between a sale and no sale. He braced himself, and reflected for a moment before dealing with the objection. If he tried to tell Gary that the premiums were no problem, he knew Gary would dig his heels in the ground. He couldn't attack him straight on. Instead, he had to defuse the objection, weaken it, strip it of all its power. The first step was to agree with Gary.

"Nobody likes premiums. I believe in insurance so much I wish it was free myself. But everything has a cost. In this case, what you are paying for is your protection. When you have this insurance, you don't ever have to worry that something might happen to Colin that will prevent you from getting your money out of this company. Why put years of your life into growing this company only to risk losing it because of a fatal tragedy?"

Gary nodded one last time. "All right. I see the value in it."

Alvin took out an application, and he and Gary filled it out. Gary then called Colin in to complete his own application. At last, Gary and Colin were Alvin's clients.

Closing time

By earning the right to proceed all along, Alvin made the close a natural result of their meeting. It was only one decision at the end of a string of smaller decisions. It was bound to happen. And when Gary made his last objection, Alvin knew to keep his cool, and respond appropriately. He defused the objection by agreeing with Gary, and then together they agreed to put the insurance in force. Throughout the meeting, Alvin was not selling to Gary, he was not standing in front of him trying to foist his products on him. Rather, he was standing beside him the whole time — helping him buy.

Best Practice Number 4: Help your prospects and clients buy

1) Establish confidence.

2) Identify your prospect's needs, wants and values.

3) Develop the solution.

4) Present the solution.

5) Close.

Get the word 'I'
out of your vocabulary
and replace it with 'we.'

Chapter 7

Best Practice Number 5: Create client capital

We saw in the last two chapters how to use the best practices of high-performing salespeople to convert selling opportunities into sales. But when you make a sale, your work with that client has only just begun. All top salespeople recognize that focusing on individual sales is not the best practice for maximizing their income and realizing their full potential. In order to grow their business, they not only focus on acquiring new clients, but on harvesting the ones that they have — selling to them again and again as their personal and business needs change. In order to realize both of these benefits, high-performing salespeople work at creating and maintaining successful long-term relationships with their clients. They invest a lot of time in what I refer to as creating client capital — the fifth best practice.

In the next chapter we'll explore how you can obtain introductions. In this chapter, we'll explore the two strategies I teach my clients that allow them to create client capital: 1) Commit to ongoing service. 2) Provide added value to your clients. Let me take you back to Rebecca's story to see how she used those two strategies to 'harvest' her client, Kirkpatrick, for additional sales.

The immortal future

Rebecca pulled her Toyota Camry out of the jammed rush hour traffic on Jones St. and into a driveway that led through a small gap in the construction site's wooden hoarding. She stopped her car in front of a chain-link gate and put it in park. In front of her a huge, dirty yellow bulldozer pushed a mound of dirt off the road. Men and women in hard hats and orange vests were gathered in groups here and there, surveying a deep hole in the ground in the middle of the site. Around the edges of the hole she could see several men cutting into the remnants of the old parking-lot surface with jack hammers. To her left the metal scaffolding of a giant crane rose twenty stories in the air, its top lost amongst the reflections of the sun bouncing off the surrounding glass skyscrapers. Her fingers trembled on the leather-covered steering wheel. Even within the air-conditioned and sound-proofed comfort of her car she could feel the vibrations of the earth movers and dump trucks rolling around the site. She wasn't sure if it was the construction or her nerves that made her shake. Lincoln Kirkpatrick was such an oddball it was impossible to predict how he would react to what she had to tell him today. She was still a few minutes early for their meeting, so, as she waited for a security guard to show up, she tried to calm her anxiety by going over the details of her plan one more time.

This was her third meeting with the eccentric Mr. Kirkpatrick. Lincoln had shocked her in their initial meeting by refusing to buy insurance to protect his family. He was obsessed with the growth of Kirkpatrick Enterprises and, although he loved his family, he felt the profits from his rapidly growing business would be enough to ensure their well-being. The man wanted to be bigger than Disney. She had finally been able to convince him to buy life insurance only by a last ditch appeal to the safety of his business. The insurance she sold him would protect against the possibility of his heirs cannibalizing the company's profits to pay the estate taxes if he died during an economic downturn. Now she was here to deliver that policy, but what Lincoln didn't know was that she had an even bigger goal for this meeting.

A hundred feet down the road she saw a short man in a blue uniform walking towards her car. He seemed unconcerned by the bustle of activity around him or the fact that her car was waiting at the gate. He walked slowly, oblivious to the dump trucks bouncing past him on their way to the far end of the site and the backhoes loudly scooping concrete rubble out of a hole to his right. While she waited, Rebecca ran through a mental checklist to make sure she was absolutely prepared for Lincoln. Although this meeting should have been a formality, just to deliver the actual paperwork for his policy, she had prepared for it as if it was a sales interview. The new idea she was going to propose could cost her the insurance she had already sold Kirkpatrick or it could double the amount of coverage he was paying for.

Rebecca's new idea

Rebecca thought back to how she had uncovered the new idea. She had made her discovery a week before, on the morning she had set aside to prepare for the delivery of Kirkpatrick's policy. With a coffee in front of her and Kirkpatrick's file laid out on her large desk, she began to follow her regular routine of reviewing his file to make sure everything was in order. Her friends often joked that she was a nervous Nellie, maybe a little obsessive, but she always took the time to check all documents for accuracy before handing them over to her clients. She had seen too many agents make themselves look foolish by delivering incomplete or incorrect policies. Some had even lost cases they thought they had already sold.

Rebecca pored over the notes she had kept. She wanted to make certain she had followed through on every promise she had made to Kirkpatrick. One of the things she had said she would do was call an accountant for an expert opinion on the estate-tax implications of the insurance. She saw that she had, in fact, faxed the results over to Kirkpatrick's office a week earlier. After checking a few more notes, Rebecca realized that she had completed everything. Kirkpatrick's policy was all in order. She leaned back, satisfied.

Rebecca then took a few minutes to walk through the delivery meeting in her head. She began running through all of the reasons why Kirkpatrick needed this policy and how it would improve his tax position. She pictured how she would tell him about the benefits this policy would provide for his family. If necessary, she would remind him that it was a much better solution to his estate problems than simply relying on his business to pay the taxes. That had been his main objection at their initial meeting.

Rebecca then moved on to the final — and most important — task in her preparation routine. Rebecca proceeded to read Kirkpatrick's biographical material again, trying to identify all of the needs he was likely to have in the future. The policy she had in front of her would fill some of his needs, but certainly not all of them. Were there any needs that could become future sales opportunities? After a couple of minutes of hard thought about Lincoln Kirkpatrick and his business, an idea began to form. Something from their very first conversation came back to her — Kirkpatrick talking about a man in his organization who would be responsible for most of the company's future growth. Rebecca realized that this man represented a huge need. This need was the crux of her new idea — it would be the focus of her delivery meeting.

The delivery

Suddenly the security guard was at her window, tapping on it with his swollen knuckles. His wrinkled face was pressed close to the glass, and she could see his lips moving. Quickly, she fumbled for the switch that would lower the window. When her nervous fingers hit the button, the window slid open a few inches. Instantly she was deafened and blinded by the roar of the machines and spray of sand that jetted into her car. The old man's gnarled face leaned closer, pressing into the gap between the window and the roof. "Go through!" he screamed above the roar. "The gate's open."

Rebecca nodded quickly and slid the window closed to shut out the din. She put the car in drive, then pulled through the gate and slowly wound her way through the workers operating cement mixers and pneumatic drills to a low trailer sitting on concrete blocks in an empty corner of the site. She parked the car, grabbed her briefcase and then paused for a second with her fingers gripping the handle on her door. I'm determined to make this sale, she told herself, then took one slow, deep breath to steady her nerves, opened the door and ran like hell across the sandy lot into the red metal trailer.

The door slammed shut behind her and she found herself in a sudden oasis of calm and silence. In front of her, smiling behind a dark wooden desk, was Lincoln Kirkpatrick. As he stood and extended his hand to say hello she noticed he was wearing a loud floral print vest over a white shirt. His black suit jacket was thrown over the back of the chair behind him. He was incongruously dressed for a day on the construction site.

"Hi, Rebecca," he said as they shook hands, "sorry to drag you out to the site just to deliver this policy, but I couldn't tear myself away from the action. Did you notice they were pouring the basement foundations when you drove in?"

"No, no I didn't," she said, taking a seat across from him.

Lincoln was too excited to sit down, instead he wandered slowly to the small window beside his desk and looked out. "Well, maybe it just looks like a big hole in the ground, but this is the first big step in putting up the largest movie-theater complex in the downtown core," he said gesturing to the construction site outside. "Twenty-five theaters, an arcade, restaurants. It's got everything!"

"That's great," Rebecca agreed. "From what I've seen today, it looks like business is booming. And, the policy you now have with our company is a good guarantee that it will carry on no matter what happens. Certainly your wife and children will be well provided for if you were to pass on. Using the substitute creditor concept we've chosen, you'll be able to retire any bank loans still outstanding at your death without any impact on the company." Reaching into her briefcase she took out an attractive leather case which contained the client copy of the policy and placed it on Kirkpatrick's desk.

"Yes, I suppose," said Lincoln, "but death is such a negative thing to focus on. I'm so caught up in the life and growth of this business — I hate being reminded that it could all come crashing down one day." He paused and began pacing the room.

"What you have done is take an important first step toward ensuring that this company will be around long after you are gone, Lincoln," Rebecca said.

"I want it to be immortal!" Lincoln laughed, whirling around to face her, a manic gleam in his eye.

"I know, I know. . . ." Rebecca said. "Last time we talked you told me all about being bigger than MGM and Disney!" This was the opening that Rebecca had been waiting for. This was the perfect opportunity to tell Lincoln her new proposal, but she had no idea how he would receive it. He was so unpredictable. She put her hand on her knee to stop her leg from shaking, then plunged right in.

"Lincoln, I think you need more insurance," she said firmly.

He stopped pacing and looked at her in surprise. "Rebecca,"

he said, "you're here delivering my policy. How could I already need more?"

"Because your company is growing so fast, Lincoln," she said. "Last time we met you told me about all of the expansion you've been doing on the Pacific Rim, right? You're opening theaters all over Asia — in Japan, Singapore, Hong Kong, everywhere."

"Sure, stagnation is death," he said with a smile. "This business is like a shark — if it stops moving it'll drown."

"And where did you say your biggest new market was?" she asked.

"Oh, India, by far," Lincoln replied. Suddenly he whirled around to face her. "Rebecca, tell me, what do you think of East Indian film?"

"What?" Rebecca said, laughing along with him. "I've never seen an Indian film. How would I know?"

"Did you know that a successful Indian film has more viewers than a Hollywood blockbuster? They're movie mad!" he said, throwing up his arms. That's why I'm opening so many Indian movie theaters this year. It's the entertainment country of the future and I'm one of the first western companies in the pool."

"So that's why you put Raji Muhindar in charge of Asian expansion?" Rebecca asked.

"You have a good memory, Rebecca Hoyle," Kirkpatrick said. "I'm impressed that you remembered his name."

Rebecca was encouraged, but she knew she needed to make an appeal to his business sense if she was going to be able to sell him the product she had in mind.

"Lincoln, I remembered Mr. Muhindar's name because when you described him to me and the role he plays in your expansion plans I realized that he was your company's Achilles' heel."

Now it was Kirkpatrick's turn to be surprised by the turn in the conversation. "What?" he asked, folding his arms and staring at her. "How can Muhindar be an Achilles' heel? He's the best man I have. He's single-handedly pulling together my Asian operations for me."

"That's exactly my point, Lincoln," Rebecca said. "How many times a month do you fly over there? Do you speak Indian, or Japanese or any of those languages? Do you understand the laws and the people well enough to open theaters on your own?"

"No, of course not," said Lincoln. "Like I said, that's why I hired

Muhindar. I don't need to go over there or get involved at all."

"So, Mr. Muhindar is a key man in your organization," Rebecca said. "But think about this. The policy that I just gave you protects your business from your death. It will ensure that your family won't have to raid Kirkpatrick Enterprise's coffers to pay your estate taxes. But you aren't the only one your business depends on. What would happen if Mr. Muhindar was to die or, even worse, to walk across the street to your competitors? Would you be able to go in and run the international business? That's the loss you're facing — your Achilles' heel. What we could do, however, is put key man insurance in place that will protect the revenues of your company until you recover from his loss."

Kirkpatrick was silent for a moment. Rebecca took a deep breath and tried to remain calm. She was scared. What if Lincoln thought she was too aggressive? In the back of her mind she half worried he might even tear up their original policy. He was very unpredictable and she had been forced to push him to make her point.

Lincoln Kirkpatrick thought for a few seconds in silence and then looked down at her without smiling. She was unable to tell which way his decision might go. "You are right about how critical expansion has become to my business," he said carefully, as if thinking out loud. "And Asia has become the hot market. With Raji's help it has become an important part of my business — that's where my future growth is."

He was silent again for a minute. He stood at the window rubbing his hand over his cheeks. Finally, he turned back to face her and said, "I guess I've never really thought through what could happen if I lost Raji. I don't have a contingency plan to speak of. We should talk further about what you can do."

Rebecca arranged another meeting with Kirkpatrick to focus solely on key man insurance on Raji Muhindar. Eventually, Kirkpatrick took out a policy that covered two years worth of Kirkpatrick Enterprise's revenue from Asian expansion. That would be enough to keep the operation afloat and profitable until Kirkpatrick could find another expansion expert and train them to fill the job. As an added bonus for Kirkpatrick and Raji, Rebecca was able to structure the key man insurance so that it also acted as a golden parachute — if Raji stayed with Kirkpatrick until he retired he would be able to claim the cash value of the policy and enjoy his retirement without financial worries. Because she was harvesting a relationship, she wasn't just making one sale, but a network of sales. The value of the relationship continued to increase for both Rebecca and Lincoln. Like any good investment, the equity grew for the benefit of all the stakeholders. Working with Raji on the key man insurance also led to additional sales which addressed Raji's personal needs. Over the next few months, Rebecca made additional sales to protect other key people in the company. She also provided group insurance and a pension plan for the employees, as well as plans for meeting the personal financial needs of key executives.

Strategy 1: Commit to ongoing service

As we just saw with Rebecca, a sale is both a beginning and an end. After the sale is closed your work is actually far from finished. When the initial sale is finished, high-performing salespeople will then shift from a selling strategy to a relationship strategy in order to go deep on that client and sell to them again and again. The key to developing and maintaining relationships with your clients is your commitment to providing first-class ongoing service.

After the sale

As with Rebecca, your first contact with a client after the sale has been made will normally be the actual delivery of the product they purchased from you. Creating client capital means that you cannot treat this delivery call as a mere formality. The low-performing salespeople who have couriers make deliveries or just drop in on clients unannounced and without a plan, squander the chance to make their next sale and to further build up client capital. I think this is because they do not understand the psychology at work after a sale has been made. Although the salesperson is probably relieved to have made a sale and is already mentally focused on their next prospect or client — worrying over their wants, needs and values — their client is now more tense than they were before they made a purchase. For the salesperson the sale is over, but for the buyer the relationship continues because the client has just made a major investment in them, both financially and emotionally. Because you were able to gain their confidence, they have taken a risk and placed their trust in you and your claims about the product. The last thing they need at that crucial time is to be abandoned, ignored or patronized. They are looking for reassurance that the expectations you built up in their mind will be met. That's why after-the-sale service is vital. Taking time to ensure that the outcome matches or exceeds the client's expectation is critical to your success. High-performing salespeople take advantage of every opportunity to provide service for their clients and make them comfortable with the product they have bought. They make delivery calls in person and do everything in their power to ensure their client's continued satisfaction.

Let's take a look at how Rebecca applied this first strategy during her product delivery meeting.

The product delivery meeting

Rebecca knew that the product delivery meeting is the first opportunity to provide service after the sale. And she also understood that it was a chance to reposition herself for future sales — that's crucial. So, she treated the product delivery interview as a sales call and prepared for it as she would any other sales meeting. She identified her objectives and then prepared herself to achieve those outcomes.

Planning for the delivery

As we saw in the story, Rebecca took some time, a week before delivering the policy, to review Lincoln's file and check his policy for accuracy. She reviewed his needs and made sure she was able to speak to how the policy's features and benefits would meet those needs. Rebecca knew that his main objection to buying life insurance had been his desire to grow his business. When preparing for the delivery she not only anticipated that objection but was able to use it as a springboard to another sale. She knew she had met his primary need for insurance, but the importance he placed on his business made her think of other sales opportunities. After investing a short time exploring what those other needs might be, she realized he had a strong need for key man insurance on Raji. That realization gave her an objective for the meeting — to reposition herself for a future sale.

Incompletions rob you of energy

Before moving on to the actual delivery meeting, Rebecca made sure that she had followed through on all of the commitments she had made to Lincoln Kirkpatrick during the first sales meeting. She understood that incompleted tasks can rob you of energy and diminish your client's confidence in you. As we saw with Alvin in Chapter 5, one of the cardinal principles of salesmanship is 'Do what you say you will do.' The danger in not following this rule is that uncompleted tasks will weigh on your mind, creating guilt and sapping your confidence. Conversely, following through on everything you promise to a client underlines your integrity. When they feel you have integrity, clients will have confidence in their decision to work with you, your relationship will be strengthened, and future sales will become possible.

Integrity

A few years before her meeting with Kirkpatrick, when her insurance business was growing rapidly, Rebecca found it hard to complete all of the small tasks that follow a sale. She was so busy trying to meet with new prospects and convert them to clients that some of the smaller steps in the sales process slipped through the cracks. Because she didn't see any immediate income from delivering a policy, she would often send her assistant around to deliver it or would just call in on a client in-between other appointments for a five-minute chat. Not only did these deliveries not generate any additional sales, they actually had a negative impact on her business. In many cases her clients would begin to doubt her commitment to servicing them and their confidence in her would drop. Her integrity was compromised. All clients want to believe they are your number-one priority. After losing two clients to other agents for exactly that reason, Rebecca committed to following through on what she said she would do, and planning and executing productive delivery calls.

The interview

When Rebecca had finished planning for her delivery meeting with Lincoln Kirkpatrick, she called him up to ask for an appointment. Unfortunately, on the day they were scheduled to meet, Lincoln called to cancel because he had to rush over to the construction site. Instead of delaying the meeting, Rebecca turned this problem into an opportunity for creating client capital. She insisted on driving out to the site and meeting with Lincoln there — demonstrating to him an impressive drive and commitment to customer service.

Managing expectations

Once inside Kirkpatrick's trailer office, Rebecca reviewed Lincoln's financial situation and made sure he understood the benefits the policy would have for him. Reviewing the sale as she did is very important for creating client capital. When she originally made the sale, Rebecca had made promises and commitments to Kirkpatrick by telling him how her product would meet his needs. She closed the gap between his expectations about the product and the reality by walking him through its features and benefits, and how they solved his problem. This built up his confidence in her and reduced the tension he felt about making the purchase. Only then, was she able to reposition herself for the next sale.

Repositioning for future sales

Repositioning for future sales requires a recalibration of your client's expectations. When Kirkpatrick first met Rebecca, he thought he was buying a single product from her, but what he found out in the delivery meeting was that she was forming a long-term relationship with him. She knew the delivery meeting was her first chance to change Lincoln's expectations of her, from an insurance agent who had sold him one product, to a financial advisor who could meet the entire array of his business and personal needs as they grew. You must make your clients aware that you will be contacting them when necessary to inform them of new products that fit their needs and, in addition, you must let them know they can always call you if their needs change.

Focus on the client

Rebecca used an approach that focused on the client. She gained an understanding of Lincoln's business and his potential loss by identifying, clarifying and intensifying his business goals. During their discussion she got him to restate the goal he had mentioned in their first sales meeting — to become immortal! Having identified that ambitious goal, she attempted to clarify what that meant to him in terms of his business. He became very excited while he was telling her about the tremendous opportunities he was capitalizing on in foreign markets. He saw his Far East expansion plans as being central to the growth and sustenance of his company. Rebecca was able to intensify that goal and make it real for him by focusing his attention on Raji Muhindar, the linchpin of his entire plan for global domination. Armed with that knowledge they were able to develop a plan for implementing key man insurance on Muhindar and protecting Kirkpatrick's business.

Rebecca was able to make that sale because she had a system that focused on her continuing relationship with Lincoln Kirkpatrick. We'll see in the next chapter how Rebecca was also able to use this system to generate a referral from Mr. Kirkpatrick and make yet another sale.

Strategy 2: Provide added value to your clients

The way that clients judge the value of a product has changed drastically over the past 25 years. Today the client is looking for more than just a product that meets their needs. They no longer rely solely on finding the best product. It is no longer enough to add up the value of a product's features, advantages and benefits. Instead, because of the tremendous competition for their attention, today's sophisticated clients take those considerations as a given and then judge value in terms of the added value the salesperson brings to the relationship.

A lesson from the computer business

A good example of this shift in consumer attitudes is the change in the way computers are now sold versus when they were first introduced in the early eighties. When microcomputers first became popular, a host of retail outlets, such as Computerland and

ComputerAge, sprung up. These stores sold their product — computers — based on its features and benefits. Since that initial computer explosion, the market has matured. Commodity pricing has increased the pressure on manufacturers and retailers alike to accept smaller and smaller margins. Consumers are no longer willing to pay anything just to own their own computer.

To avoid being labeled commodity merchants, smart retailers don't sell computers and software, they provide business solutions. The customer buys a solution that increases productivity and profits. The customer assesses the value of the solution based upon the advantage it provides to their business, not just the price. The more innovative organizations offer a contract which allows the user to upgrade their systems as their needs change over time. When they run out of memory, decide they need a CD-ROM, sound or video, the retailer is able to provide added value. As a result, the client sees the vendor as an ongoing resource solving new problems as they arise.

Added value

As a sales professional you must follow the lead of the innovative vendors and provide similar added value to your clients. An added value is best described as what you do over and above what is expected of you. In order to be a high-performing salesperson you need to differentiate yourself from your competitors by adding value to your clients.

In my career, I have worked with many clients who were excellent at adding value to their client's business and translating that value into sales. Rebecca's target market is business owner/managers. Prior to becoming an insurance professional she was a bank manager for many years and dealt with business owners everyday. She often went out to their sites to examine their businesses and over the years came to truly understand the issues they faced. After she started selling insurance to that same market, she was able to add a great deal of value by sending her business owner/manager clients financial information and educational updates that addressed issues she knew they faced. By sending them articles on collateral for business loans, buy-sell agreements, retirement plans and group benefits, she positioned herself as an expert on their financial affairs and a good resource for solving their problems. As a result, when they realized they had insurance needs they came to her.

As we saw in chapter 3, Tony Henderson was able to add value to his prospects' and clients' companies by delivering seminars on issues that were relevant to their businesses, such as employee benefits. Alvin, who we met in chapter 2, added value to his clients by holding concept lunches at which his clients could meet and talk to a variety of experts from his network about a specific topic — retirement planning, for instance. In chapter 10, we'll explore this idea even further. I'll show you how you can utilize external resources, such as accountants, lawyers, actuaries, and human resource specialists, who are part of your network of experts, to further add value to your clients' business.

'We' not 'I'

By committing to ongoing service and providing added value, high-performing salespeople dramatically increase the number of sales they can make to every client. What those two strategies do is change your approach from selling one product to managing a life-long relationship. I have found that the key to making that transition is to get the word 'I' out of your vocabulary and replace it with 'we.' 'We' suggests a combined effort and bond between seller and buyer versus the more adversarial traditional selling role. If you can create that bond you will be living the fifth best practice — create client capital.

Best Practice Number 5: Create client capital

1) Commit to ongoing service.
2) Provide added value to your clients.

She thought of the confusing
maze of streets winding around
the base of the giant towers —
the traffic and people going about
their business in perpetual shadow. . . .
In Hong Kong she could take
her career to an entirely
new level — but in order
to do that she needed to
close one crucial case.

Chapter 8

Best Practice Number 6: Obtain introductions

I n the last chapter we saw how high-performing salespeople create client capital to harvest sales from their existing clients. But high performers do more than just harvest their existing clients; they constantly seek out new clients. And the way they do that is by utilizing best practice number 6 — obtain introductions.

The difference between referrals and introductions

Before we get started, I'd like to discuss the difference between referrals and introductions. Most salespeople are trained to grow their business by obtaining referrals, but, as David Cowper, author of *Breakthrough*, pointed out to me, he and other high-performers grow their business not by getting referrals but by gaining introductions.

When a salesperson gets a referral it is usually just the name, telephone number and address of one of their client's friends or colleagues. By contrast, an introduction is an actual meeting between the salesperson, their client and the prospect their client is recommending them to. For instance, when Alvin was just starting out, he would ask his clients for referrals. Frequently all they would do is write a name and phone number down on a slip of paper and hand it over to him. Only occasionally would those new prospects turn into clients. However, later in his career, once he'd learned to ask for introductions, he was able to create the opportunity to meet in person with his client and new prospect. He was able to develop many of those introductions into new clients.

High-performing salespeople prefer introductions over referrals because they instill a greater sense of confidence in the prospect and, as we saw in best practice number 3 — understand how people make decisions — all decisions are confidence based. What Alvin learned is that it is easier to graduate a prospect into a client through an introduction than through a referral.

In this chapter we'll explore the two strategies for obtaining introductions: 1) Make yourself referable. 2) Utilize the 8-step process for obtaining introductions. Let me take you back to Rebecca once again to show you how she used these two strategies to obtain introductions and grow her business.

Foreign affairs

Rebecca reclined her seat as far back as it would go and stretched her legs out ahead of her. It had been three years since she had last taken a plane anywhere and she was excited. She lay her head back on the seat rest and took a deep breath to relax. She had certainly never flown anywhere to meet a prospect before — she guessed that most agents hadn't. The case she was about to enter would be a test of her new approach to growing her business by obtaining introductions, rather than through mere referrals. She was anxious to see what difference a personal introduction made. Out the window to her right she had an unbroken view of the sun reflecting off the endless expanse of the bright, green Pacific Ocean. In front of her, Bruce Willis and an old character actor she didn't recognize talked soundlessly on the movie screen, but she wasn't in the mood for a film — she was too wound up. The headphones she needed to hear their dialogue were still stowed in the overhead bin along with her briefcase. There was no way she could pay attention to a movie or get any work done. She couldn't stop thinking about landing in Hong Kong and what awaited her there. She sipped her diet cola and silently watched the water rush past miles below.

As she relaxed, she began to daydream about Hong Kong. She had seen pictures of the tall skyscrapers packed tightly together around the harbor. She thought of the confusing maze of streets winding around the base of the giant towers — the traffic and people going about their business in perpetual shadow. Her leg shook nervously as she considered the possibilities ahead of her. She knew this city had a thriving economy. In Hong Kong she could take her career to an entirely new level — but in order to do that she needed to close one crucial case.

The final approach

A soft chime from the cabin PA system startled her out of her reverie. The copilot announced that they were beginning their descent into Hong Kong and gave instructions for stowing luggage and fastening seat belts. As she looked out the window, the plane banked to the south, and as the wing dropped, Hong Kong harbor came into view. In the murky brown water, hundreds of sail boats, old motor boats and rusting tugs were jammed together. On the shore, a tight crush of glass skyscrapers stretched up towards her, spilling up the steep hillside behind the city. It was exactly as she pictured it — twice as dense as New York and probably even more hectic. It was the kind of place where fortunes could be won or lost by someone with brains and determination. Very shortly after the plane landed she would know if she had what it took to compete for its global business.

With that thought, a knot formed in Rebecca's stomach. This was her final approach. And the one prospect that everything hinged upon was Johnny Huang. That was who she was here to see. She had met Huang briefly, a week earlier, on the other side of the ocean. And now she was landing in his city, having traveled six thousand miles to sell him insurance. It had seemed ridiculous to some of the other agents she worked with, but Rebecca knew exactly what she was doing. She had a new target market — the international business owner/manager and she had a new approach for developing a network to get her into that target market. Johnny was the first prospect she had acquired in the Far East using her new approach. He was young, a 31-year-old hustler, and on the verge of major financial success if he played his cards right. He was born and raised in the same city as Rebecca, but had married a woman from Hong Kong. He split his life between the two cities. He had already made a small fortune from the three nightclubs he owned — two in Hong Kong and one in San Francisco — but could easily become hugely rich in the near future if several of the deals he was involved in worked out. He would be a very lucrative sale, but, even more importantly, if she could convert him from a prospect to a client on this trip, the door to Asia would swing wide open. He would become a center of influence for her in this massive new market.

A new approach for obtaining introductions

After Rebecca had disembarked and made her way through customs, she stepped through the sliding glass doors and out into a melee — hundreds of men, women and children shouted wildly to get their relatives' attention. Suitcases and knapsacks were strewn everywhere. Children chased each other noisily through the tangled maze of their parents' legs. In the center of the throng, she saw the man who might change her career — Johnny Huang. He was unmistakable, standing quietly with his arms folded across his chest, wearing black pants and a short sleeve Hawaiian print shirt. When he saw Rebecca struggling through the crowd with her bags he broke into a smile and rushed to help her.

Although they had only met once before, briefly, Johnny treated Rebecca like an old friend. He shook her hand warmly, grabbed her luggage and pushed his way through the crowd to his waiting car. The entire way back into town he talked incessantly — about his city, his business and what they might be able to do together. Rebecca began to suspect that her new approach for obtaining introductions was working better than she'd ever imagined.

She spent the next week hurrying in and out of appointments with Johnny. Rebecca knew that if she could close this one case her clientele would quickly expand into a global network because Johnny would be able to introduce her to his contacts all over Asia. This trip was vital to her future as a salesperson, so she did everything she could to gain a complete understanding of Johnny's business and close the deal. She toured his nightclubs with him, met his partners, spent hours going through his financial statements, even looked at plans for a new resort in mainland China that he was hoping to build. They visited restaurants and hotels where he knew people — all of them business men and women in similar situations, with similar issues. The opportunities for her were enormous.

By the end of the week, Rebecca had a thorough understanding of Johnny Huang's needs, wants and values. At one of their final meetings, she spent a lot of time very clearly exposing his risks. As she spoke, his face fell. For the first time all week Johnny stopped smiling. He knew he was heavily in debt with no insurance to offset the risk, but when she explained in painful detail what could happen to his business in a worst-case scenario he was mortified. After that, closing the case was a mere formality. When Johnny saw the benefits of the insurance solutions that she was offering, he wasted no time in signing the applications. Rebecca had closed the case — she was ecstatic!

During the flight home, Rebecca went over in her mind how she had managed to gain an appointment with Johnny Huang. She would never have been able to do it if she hadn't used her new approach for obtaining prospects. And she never would have flown to Hong Kong. She was filled with excitement. This was the beginning of a new stage in her career. With her new approach she figured she would be able to more than double her revenue in the next year alone. And it had all started with Lincoln Kirkpatrick, her movie-theater-developer client.

Getting the appointment with Johnny Huang

She remembered how, on a Tuesday afternoon a few weeks earlier, Lincoln Kirkpatrick had met Rebecca at the door to his office. He smiled broadly, shook her hand and then led her inside. She was there for a very important reason, but Lincoln didn't know it. As he took a seat in his large, studded leather chair, Rebecca noticed a new photograph on the wall behind him. It was a color shot of a dozen oriental men in hard hats and boots posed in front of a massive concrete building. In front of those people an Indian man and an oriental man, both in suits and hard hats, shook hands. The building didn't look like a movie theater to Rebecca, it was far too large. From the photo it looked like it was ten stories or more. And in the background she could see nothing but trees and empty lawn. Not the best location for a theater she thought.

Putting the picture out of her mind, Rebecca settled down to business. She was here to find some new prospects.

"Lincoln," she began, "I'm here to pick up the signed

applications for the Riojas and Benedito policies, but before we do that, I wonder if we could talk about something else for a second."

"Sure, Rebecca," he replied, with a laugh. "I've always got time for you. I'd bet you've got half my company tied up in policies, by now. . . ."

"Yes, that's right," she said, smiling. "We've done several cases together now, and actually I wanted to see how you felt about the work we've done."

"What do you mean?" he asked.

"Well, are you happy with the service I've provided? Do you think the policies we've chosen solve your problems?" Rebecca said. She needed to confirm that he was confident in her abilities before she proceeded to her real purpose for this visit.

"Sure, sure I'm happy," Lincoln said. "I hate the premiums but I certainly wouldn't have bought the policies if I didn't think I needed the protection. And, as for the service, it's unusually good. Frankly, I've been approached by a lot of salespeople over the years — being a developer means financial salespeople are kind of an occupational hazard — but I didn't buy anything from them. If you remember, when you first came to me, I tried to shoo you out the door. I thought I could rely on the profits from my business to take care of my family. But you were the only one who could show me the risks I was taking in a way that made sense to me. I'm happy with what we've done."

Asking for introductions

Rebecca paused and looked him in the eye. "I'm glad to hear that, Lincoln. I take great pride in what I do and I especially enjoy working with you. But, the truth is — I need your help."

Lincoln's eyebrows shot up. "What? What kind of help?"

"Lincoln," Rebecca began, "in order for me to continue to grow my business, I need to meet quality people to whom I can offer my services. The best way for me to meet potential clients is through someone like yourself, who has the qualities I'm looking for in my clients."

"Oh, jeez, I thought you needed a kidney or something," Lincoln said. "I'm glad to hear it's not anything too serious, but I don't know how much I can help you. You've already insured all my key people, and you're even doing the group plan here."

"Let me be more specific about what I'm looking for then," Rebecca said. "The types of individuals I want to work with are entrepreneurs, executives and professionals. Typically, they are busy people like yourself who are taking risks in their business. They are successful, affluent, intelligent and responsible. Who can you think of, not including the people we've already insured, that fit those criteria? Maybe they're people in your circle of friends and acquaintances."

"Intelligent, responsible, wealthy. . . . Hmmm, besides me I'm not sure." Lincoln leaned back into the studded chair and thought for a moment. "How about Howie Marantz, he owns Cloverleaf Chemicals. Their office is right here in town. They do well. They make lawn fertilizer and sprays and stuff."

Rebecca didn't really think Marantz was her type of client. He was childless and she'd heard he was trying to sell his company. She wrote down his name, but she knew she had to dig deeper if she was going to uncover the prospects that would take her to the next level.

"Lincoln, what about some of the people your company does business with?" she asked. "You're expanding so fast and I know you have a lot of joint venture partners. They don't have to be in town — just throw out some names."

Lincoln looked around the room, as if searching for an answer. When he saw the picture of the construction site to his right — the one Rebecca had noticed when she first came in — his eyes lit up. "Hey, how about Johnny Huang? He sure isn't local, but he definitely fits your criteria. He's the guy in this picture with that ugly flowered shirt under his suit," he said pointing to the oriental man in the front row. "He's standing beside Raji Muhindar."

Rebecca's heart raced. Johnny Huang sounded much more promising. She was definitely interested in expanding her practice into global business insurance, that's why she had been so thrilled to get Lincoln Kirkpatrick as a client. With his Asian operations expanding so rapidly she had known he was sure to be a center of influence for that market.

"So, could you tell me a little bit about Mr. Huang? What kind of guy is he? What exactly does he do?" she asked.

Deep into the mud bath

Lincoln laughed, "Oh, Johnny's crazy, that's for sure. But he's got a great head for business. He's a young guy, I guess you can tell that from the picture. I think he's 31. But he already owns two nightclubs in Hong Kong that are really hot right now. And, he just opened another one in San Francisco two months ago. That's how I met him. I was in town for a conference and happened to wander in there one night with a few friends. He made us all feel real welcome and by the end of the night we'd exchanged business cards and were talking about ways to work together. Anyway, he called me the next time he was over here and told me about this new venture he had going with a group of businessmen from Germany who he'd met in his Hong Kong club. They wanted to open a spa/resort in China.

"At first I laughed, I didn't think the Chinese would be too interested in mud baths. But that's Johnny for you, it's a perfect idea for him. He always takes the least likely proposition and makes it into a winner. Anyway, that picture on my wall was taken just after they finished construction on the new resort. It opens next month."

Rebecca was impressed. If nothing else, Johnny would be exciting to work with. But she needed more information on him to decide if he would actually be a profitable prospect. "It sounds like Johnny's a smart guy, with a lot of money in his future, Lincoln," she said. "Let me ask you, is he married? Does he have kids?"

Lincoln smiled across the desk at Rebecca, "He sure does. I met his wife when they were here last time. They have a beautiful two year old son."

"And, how often is he here?"

"Well, since we've been working together he's been flying over every few weeks — to see to his club and to discuss how we'll move forward on this resort we've built."

Rebecca knew she had a perfect new prospect — if she could enlist Lincoln's help. She knew that it would be pointless to phone a busy man like Johnny Huang out of the blue and introduce herself. He would never agree to meet with her.

"Lincoln," she started, "the likelihood of Mr. Huang meeting with me is directly related to the confidence he places in your judgment. If he values your recommendation and believes that you are concerned about his interests, then he is likely to at least listen to my story. Would you have any objections to introducing me to him the next time he is here?"

Lincoln looked a little startled. "Rebecca, I. . . ," he stuttered, "when he is here we have very little time and always have a lot to discuss. I could phone him for you if you like and then you could try to get an appointment with him."

"No," Rebecca said, "I need to meet him when he's with you. That way you can introduce us in person and he will make a positive connection. I want him to know that you have enough confidence in me to recommend me in person. When are you meeting him next?"

Lincoln checked his day planner on his desk. "Ahh, Thursday at one. Then I believe he has a flight to catch at 4, so I'm sure he'll be in a hurry."

Rebecca cut him off before he could say no, "Lincoln, that's not a problem. I'll be here at five-to-one. When Mr. Huang shows up I'll be waiting in here and as he walks in you can introduce me as we pass. It'll be natural and I promise it will waste none of your time."

Realizing that he had met an irresistible force, Lincoln agreed to her plan. Before she left, Rebecca picked up the applications she had originally come for and, on her way out, thanked him for his help and promised to keep him informed of her progress.

Johnny Huang in the flesh

Two days later, Lincoln introduced Rebecca to Johnny Huang as she had suggested. Johnny had smiled graciously and shook her hand. As they stood for a second in the doorway to the office, Lincoln told Johnny about the policies she had created for him and his key people and explained how valuable he thought Rebecca was to his business. Johnny seemed impressed by what Lincoln had to say and when Rebecca offered him a business card, he asked her to call him in Hong Kong.

When Rebecca followed up with Johnny she found out that he would now be spending the next six months at home in Hong Kong because his wife was expecting their second child shortly. He was anxious to put insurance in force not only for his business but for his rapidly expanding family. The only thing to do was to fly over there to meet him.

On the way home from Hong Kong

Now, only two short weeks had passed and Johnny Huang was no longer a prospect, he was her client. As her plane cruised silently through the pitch black night over the Pacific, Rebecca rolled restlessly in her seat. She was too excited to sleep. The new approach for obtaining introductions that she used with Lincoln Kirkpatrick had paid off with an introduction to Johnny Huang. And she had been able to convert that opportunity into a sale and the promise of many more in the Far East. As she looked out at the full moon that shone brightly on the horizon, she thought she would have to phone Lincoln the second she got home and thank him for the introduction and the new opportunities he had opened up for her. She knew he'd be happy that he could help both her and his new partner, Johnny Huang.

What she referred to as her 'new approach to growing her business' was really the sixth best practice — obtain introductions. Had she not been able to utilize the two strategies that make up this best practice, Rebecca never would have had the opportunity to meet Johnny Huang. As mentioned earlier, these two strategies are: 'Make yourself referable,' and 'Utilize the 8-step process for obtaining introductions.' As you could see in her encounter with Johnny Huang, introductions are crucial to meeting your ideal clients and growing your business. Before we explore the two strategies that enabled Rebecca to obtain introductions and see how they relate to the Johnny Huang case, let's look at why obtaining introductions is so important.

The importance of introductions

Introductions are a way of positively positioning yourself with your prospects so that they are confident in your abilities and can be converted into clients. Let me show you what I mean.

Positioning

Positioning refers to those activities which create a favorable impression *before* you meet a prospect. In a perfect world, if you were perfectly positioned to your target market, you would be able to sit in your office and prospects would be so impressed with your products and service that they would call you up looking to make a purchase. That would be extremely positive positioning. However, if you sit around waiting for prospects to call, you're likely to starve before you grow rich.

At the other end of the positioning spectrum, you could make cold calls. However, whenever you call a prospect who has never heard of you, they are likely to be thinking three things — 'I don't know who you are,' 'I don't know how your products or services can help me with my problems,' and 'I don't know how I can benefit from a meeting with you.' In short they will be defensive and concerned with maintaining the status quo. This is very definitely an example of negative positioning.

The path of least resistance

I believe that the closest many agents will come to perfect positive positioning is an introduction from someone the prospect knows and respects. I say this because, when you make a cold call, you are following the path of greatest resistance. You have to deal with your own discomfort over calling someone who is likely to reject you. Then you have to overcome the prospect's negative reaction to your call. It is emotionally taxing, to say the least.

Introductions establish confidence

Unlike cold calls, however, obtaining an introduction follows the path of least resistance because you are able to hitchhike on the credibility one of your existing clients has with the new prospect. This credibility is a lever that creates much greater influence with a new prospect than you would otherwise enjoy.

When you obtain an introduction you now have something in common with your new prospect — the client who referred you. And, the more you have in common with another person, the easier it is to establish rapport, which, as we saw in chapter 6, is crucial to helping your prospects and clients buy from you. Remember, all decisions are confidence based. If your prospect has confidence in your client, that confidence is transferred to you.

Now that you understand the importance of obtaining introductions, let's look at how Rebecca was able to use the first strategy to meet Johnny Huang.

Strategy 1: Make yourself referable

What Rebecca and all high-performing salespeople understand is that you may make a sale to a client if you follow the first 5 best practices, but you won't get introductions unless you make yourself referable.

Creating client capital

In order to make yourself referable you need to develop a good relationship with your client. As we saw in chapter 7, it is not enough to make one sale to a client and then move on to the next challenge. Instead, you need to create client capital so that you can sell to that client again and again over the course of their lifetime and also so that you can use them as a center of influence and obtain introductions.

Rebecca understood this best practice and put it into action in her dealings with Lincoln. As we saw in the last chapter, she made a commitment to ongoing service and added value to Lincoln's business. She took the time to hand-deliver his policy, and was able to add value by becoming a resource for him regarding financial products that could help his business. This not only enabled her to make additional sales, but it also improved his perception of her value to his business. When you create client capital, you and your client form a bond. As a result, they will not be embarrassed by your actions and will be confident in your abilities. In this chapter, we have seen how Rebecca was able to trade on the bond created by client capital and obtain an introduction from Lincoln.

Strategy 2: Utilize the 8-step process for obtaining introductions

Now let's look at the 8-step process I have developed for obtaining introductions from your clients and how Rebecca was able to use this process to get an introduction to Johnny Huang from Lincoln Kirkpatrick.

Step 1: Confirm your client's confidence in you

The first step in obtaining introductions from your clients is to confirm their confidence in you. When Rebecca met Lincoln Kirkpatrick in order to obtain introductions from him, the first thing she did was ask him how he felt about the work they had done together up to that point. What she was trying to do was confirm his confidence in her abilities and the products he had purchased.

Using framing to obtain introductions

In order to overcome any doubts Lincoln might have about making an introduction for her, Rebecca used framing to ease his fears. Framing, as we discussed in chapter 6, refers to the way in which information is presented. The way Rebecca framed her relationship with Lincoln was to remind him of the work they had done together so far. She knew that he would be happy with the service she had given him and that he had to be pleased with her products because he had bought several key person policies from her as their relationship grew over time.

Using framing to build confidence is important because clients will always judge whether or not to make an introduction for you based on the consequences and benefits that introduction would have for them. For example, if a client believes that the consequence of making an introduction is that it will alienate the friend or colleague they are introducing you to, they will be reluctant to do so. That's because people are risk averse. Their primary consideration is the avoidance of risk. So, you have to eliminate the risk and highlight the benefits they will gain from making an introduction for you.

Risk averse clients

Let me show you what I mean when I say people are risk averse. I have a client named Peter, a young agent who has been in the insurance business for two years. He has no problem asking his clients for introductions, but he never actually gets them. Why? Because he's not referable. Unfortunately, he is always nervous when dealing with his existing clients. He has a hard time selling to them because he can't keep quiet. He blurts out information at the wrong time, doesn't give his clients time to think about a decision and as a result he loses cases he should have won. But, even worse than losing single sales, is the fact that he is also losing opportunities to grow his business because of his inability to gain introductions. His nervous personality is so annoying to clients that they would be afraid to introduce him to their friends and colleagues. They fear that their long-time friends, who they have immense credibility with, would call them up and say, "Who was that freak you sicked on me?" Peter fails to understand the most important aspect of obtaining introductions: your clients will only recommend you and introduce you to others if they have complete confidence in your abilities and enjoy working with you. That's why the first step in the 8-step process is to confirm your client's confidence in you.

Step 2: Ask for help

When Rebecca had established that Kirkpatrick was confident in her abilities, she moved on to the next step in obtaining introductions. That next step is to say the four most moving words that a salesperson can ever speak to a client, "I need your help." Opening yourself up to your client and exposing your need for their help will strike a sympathetic note in them.

Having declared her need, Rebecca then explained to Lincoln that she was looking for people to whom she could offer her services. The idea of serving people is a powerful one. Let me show you why.

How to position yourself as referable

What my client Peter should have done in the example I outlined in step 1 was think of his interaction with the client in an entirely different way. Peter approached his clients with the attitude that he needed to talk them into buying something. This aggressive approach made him nervous. Instead, Peter should have thought of himself as a 'server,' whose sole function is to help his clients solve their problems. If you are helping your clients, rather than taking advantage of them, and your products are offering good value, it will only be natural for you to ask for introductions. If Peter's clients benefit from his service, he can be confident that their friends will as well.

Unfortunately, salespeople like Peter often don't ask for introductions even though they have such obvious benefits. Many salespeople are uncomfortable with the concept of prospecting because they don't like to ask others to help them in their work. What they don't understand is that most people consider being asked to help a great compliment and are only too happy to oblige. That's what Rebecca did to great effect with Lincoln. If you position yourself in this way, your clients will be more comfortable and so will you.

Step 3: Describe your ideal client

In her conversation with Lincoln Kirkpatrick, Rebecca was very careful to tell him exactly what she was looking for in a prospect. She knew that Lincoln was unlikely to introduce her to the people she needed to meet — her ideal clients — if he didn't know what characteristics they had in common. When you describe your ideal client to your prospect, you make it easy for them to help you.

Step 4: Help your client identify potential prospects for you

Sometimes, even when you have been explicit about your criteria for a new prospect, your client may have difficulty identifying suitable candidates for you. In Rebecca's case, Lincoln had first suggested Howie Marantz, but Rebecca knew he would not make a good prospect. Instead of settling for a poor candidate she knew would never become a client, Rebecca tried to elaborate and further define her criteria for Lincoln. She told him to think about people he worked with on joint ventures. She reassured him that potential prospects didn't even have to live in the same city. That was when Kirkpatrick was able to come up with the name she needed — Johnny Huang.

Feed Categories

You can use what I call 'feed categories' to help your clients identify suitable candidates for you. A feed category is any person or group of people who share a demographic or psychographic profile. Some examples of good questions that expose feed categories would be:

"What about the people you work with?" "Who are some of the other successful owner/managers you work with?" "Who is your closest friend?" "Who is the most successful person you know?" Asking these types of questions will unblock your client's mind and help them to generate a list of potential prospects for you.

Step 5: Qualify your prospects

Once you have obtained a number of names, you begin to qualify each prospect by obtaining as much information about them as possible. In Rebecca's case she already knew that Howie Marantz was childless and would not make a good prospect so she didn't probe any further.

Your clients and centers of influence help you identify your prospect's interests

As soon as Rebecca recognized potential in Johnny Huang, she began asking Lincoln a series of questions designed to qualify Johnny as a high-grade prospect. She needed to know if he was married and how often he traveled to their city. In addition, if your client has not already given you the information, you may need to ask how old your potential prospect is, how their business is doing right now, how well your client knows them. You need to know whether or not they meet your criteria for an ideal client. The more you learn about your potential prospect, the more easily you'll be able to create common bonds when you meet.

Keep in mind that good communication is the key to all interpersonal relationships. When asking the questions outlined in this 8-step process, always allow your client plenty of time to think and answer. Don't get nervous and rush them like Peter.

Using timing to obtain introductions

Another important reason to question your client about their friend's interests and current situation is that someone's circumstances will often affect their decision to buy. A decision to buy a financial product is most often circumstance or event-driven. For example, a prospect who is experiencing a significant change in their life, such as a marriage, the birth of a child, a promotion, the purchase of a new home, or starting a business is typically more receptive to a meeting with a financial advisor.

Clients or centers of influence can provide you with information that will highlight problems faced by the person they will introduce you to. You can use this information to your advantage if you are able to address your prospect's concerns at a time when they are receptive and willing to listen.

Step 6: Ask for an introduction

Once you have a number of names and have qualified them, the next step is to enlist your client's help in contacting your prospect. When Rebecca realized she wanted an introduction to Johnny she explained to Lincoln why she needed him to help her.

Let others describe your capabilities so that your reputation precedes you

Rebecca wanted Lincoln to make a point of telling Johnny how valuable she was to him and how necessary her products were. On the strength of such a positive recommendation she knew Johnny would be likely to listen to her because, as we saw in chapter 5, all decisions are confidence based. Johnny had confidence in Lincoln because they did business together. Lincoln transferred this trust to Rebecca when he positioned her as a valuable financial advisor and not just another salesperson.

Referrals versus introductions revisited

At this stage of the 8-step process you may run into trouble with a client who is willing to make a phone call on your behalf or suggest a name for you to call, but doesn't want to make an introduction. Many clients will agree to making a phone call but that's not good enough. As you saw with Rebecca, she refused to let Lincoln get away with that. She needed an introduction and she asked for it. Sometimes you can and must be firm with your clients when making such requests. In Rebecca's case she had already solidly established Lincoln's confidence in her and so she was not afraid of offending him by insisting on an introduction.

One of the best networkers in the business is David Cowper. He does not finish his sales meetings with a request for his client to refer him to a friend or colleague. Instead, he asks them to put a call into the new prospect and organize a lunch so they can get to know each other. David Cowper realizes that if one of his clients introduces him to a new prospect personally rather than just referring him, his chances of making that prospect a client are much greater. As he says, 'The phone book contains millions of referrals, but what are they worth? Get me an introduction, instead."

Step 7: Thank your client

After securing Lincoln Kirkpatrick's help with Johnny Huang, Rebecca made sure to thank him before leaving his office. This is a very important step because you must keep in mind how badly you need your client's influence and credibility to work for you — without their introduction, you would be just another stranger. A 'Thank you' will go a long way to continuing your relationship with your client and maintaining their goodwill.

Step 8: Keep your client informed

On the plane ride back from Hong Kong Rebecca was so excited she couldn't sleep. It was then that she decided to phone Lincoln as soon as she got home to fill him in on her experiences with his business partner, Johnny Huang. She knew it was important to update Lincoln. She wanted to thank him, and let him know she was able to help his friend. The fact that Johnny made the decision to do business with Rebecca would affirm for Lincoln the value of having Rebecca as an advisor. Lincoln would also benefit from the new relationship Rebecca had with Johnny, because both were now in his debt. He could be assured of even better service from Rebecca in the future.

As a final note, whenever you are updating your client, remember to respect your new client's confidentiality.

Summary: expand your referral base

Now that you understand how to make yourself referable and how to use the 8-step process for obtaining introductions, you can use those two strategies to expand your business. In order to realize the full potential of your market and harvest as many sales as possible from your clients, you will need to concentrate on using those strategies to obtain new prospects — you will need to keep the pipeline full. This is the surest way to grow your business dramatically year after year.

In order to grow as fast as possible, I always tell my clients to keep two things in mind: first, ask for introductions on a daily basis; and second, develop centers of influence who regularly provide you with the names of qualified prospects. If, by doing those two things, you can develop a habit of consistently asking for introductions from satisfied clients and converting those introductions into sales, you will have mastered the sixth best practice of high-performing salespeople.

Best Practice Number 6: Obtain introductions

1) Make yourself referable.
2) Utilize the 8-step process for obtaining introductions.

He ran around like a scalded cat,
going back and forth between appointments,
couriering many of his own packages,
sitting on the phone with underwriters,
and trying frantically to keep
on top of his mounting backlog
of telephone messages.

Chapter 9

Best Practice Number 7: Delegate

Mastery of the first six best practices will make you a superb salesperson. But unless you also master the seventh best practice — delegate — your growth will be limited. I say this because as soon as you begin utilizing the first six practices, you will find that your ability to grow is largely dependent on the amount of time you are able to spend using those very practices to develop relationships with your clients and prospects. And that's what best practice number 7 is all about — freeing up your time so that you can leverage the first six practices to their fullest. Instead of being a superb salesperson for 50% or 75% of your working day, delegation allows you to be a superb salesperson 100% of the time.

In this chapter we'll take a look at three strategies for effective delegation: 1) Delegate to other people. 2) Delegate to technology. 3) Build an organization. I'd like to begin our exploration of these strategies by telling you another story from Tony's career that took place two years ago.

D-day

It was late evening on the second Sunday in March, and Tony sat in the study of his house, reading quietly, trying to enjoy the last few moments of the weekend. His three young kids were sound asleep in their bedrooms, and his wife was getting ready for bed. He had another chapter in his book to read and he was determined to finish it. It was a whodunit novel, and he knew there was no way he'd be able to get a decent night's sleep without finding out who, in fact, did it. At around 10:30 he closed the book and leaned back in his reading chair, relieved that the mystery was finally solved.

As he sat there, contemplating the book for a few moments

longer, his mind began to wander restlessly. Now that the novel was finished, he could no longer escape what was concerning him. He had been trying not to think about it all weekend; he knew that worrying wouldn't help. But Monday morning loomed ominously — he couldn't escape it any longer.

"Tony," his wife, Cathy, whispered from the door.

"Yes," he replied, in a muffled tone.

"Are you coming to bed?"

"In a few minutes."

He listened to his wife's footsteps pad across the carpeted floor. The hallway beyond the study suddenly darkened as the master-bedroom light went out. A silence descended upon the house. Tony's mind was now completely filled with the thoughts he had been avoiding — his concerns about the coming week. In five days, he would know whether he had managed to pull it off or not. If he could, his intention of taking his team and himself to a higher level would be realized. He was excited about the next few days, but what bothered him was the small amount of time he had to accomplish everything. He had five days, not a second longer. Next Friday he was leaving with his family for two weeks vacation. Everything had to be finished by then. All his anxiety had been prompted by a brief meeting he had with his assistant, Gillian, just before the weekend. He closed his eyes and replayed their conversation.

The $2-million year

It was just before five o'clock when Gillian buzzed him on the intercom. "Tony," she said, "I've got some exciting news."

"I'd love to hear it," he replied.

"Okay, I'll be right over."

Gillian, a woman in her mid 30s, stepped into Tony's office, and sat down in the chair in front of his desk.

"What have you got?" Tony asked, anxious for the news.

Gillian slid a sheet of paper across his blotter, and Tony glanced down at it. It was the following week's schedule of appointments for the entire office, which included a brief analysis by Gillian. Everyone referred to it as the Weekly Hotsheet. When Tony's gaze fell to the bottom of the page, his eyes bulged out. Gillian watched his reaction and smiled in delight.

Tony had hired Gillian as his senior assistant financial planner four weeks ago. Gillian was the latest acquisition in his plan to build his business. Seven years before, he had been a one-man operation, doing everything on his own. Then, gradually, over the years, he had grown, first by hiring an administrative assistant, then by hiring two customer service people, a marketing support person, two junior salespeople, and a full-time receptionist. Including himself, there were now nine people in total in his office. And he no longer just sold mutual funds. He had acquired his insurance license two years before and now ran a full-service financial planning operation, advising clients on risk management, their investments, retirement plans, insurance portfolios, etc. Tony was particularly excited about hiring Gillian. She was an expert financial planner and he would be able to unload a great deal of work on her shoulders, freeing him up to grow the business even bigger.

Before joining Tony's company, Gillian had worked for five years as an insurance agent for a large insurance company, and before that she had practiced as a chartered accountant. She was a brilliant financial analyst, and was a whiz with the latest software packages. One of the things she offered to do for Tony was to put together a synopsis of the upcoming appointments using a new program she had just learned. Included in the synopsis was a projection of the total commissions at stake for the following weeks. And that was what Tony was looking at now. The projection was $40,987.00. Tony's heart was thumping wildly. He looked up from the page. Gillian was grinning. They both knew exactly what that figure meant.

When Tony first met with Gillian before hiring her, he explained that he was looking for someone who could help take the annual gross revenue of the office from just over $1.5 million to over $2 million a year. For the few weeks prior to Gillian's arrival, Tony's office had been earning a total revenue of roughly $30,000 a week. To reach the $2-million mark, Tony knew he had to push their average weekly revenue to close to $40,000. He had never been able to do that. Now, looking down at the following week's projection, he knew he had his first chance. If they managed to close all of their cases next week, the office would be on its way to a $2-million year.

"Tony, Tony," Cathy said.

Tony shook his head suddenly. Cathy was standing in front of him wrapped snugly in her robe.

"Aren't you coming to bed, dear?" she said.

He must have been completely lost in thought. He hadn't heard her come down the hall at all.

"Are you okay?" she asked.

"Sure," he responded, rising from his chair now. "Just preoccupied. What time is it?"

"Almost eleven."

"Jeez," Tony sighed. They walked hand-in-hand down the hallway.

A few minutes later, Tony was lying beside his wife in bed. She had fallen right back to sleep, her chest rising and falling with slow, deep breaths. He thought once more about the week's projection. A final pang of anxiety seized him. He wanted to do it so badly. He wanted to be sitting on a plane the following Friday with his wife and kids, knowing his team had reached a new level of achievement. But before that could happen, his team would have to work together effectively to close the biggest week the office had ever had. He reassured himself that they could do it. He had been preparing for years for such a week. He had hired half-a-dozen people, invested tens of thousands of dollars in computer equipment, and built a complex organization for the purpose of being able to handle such an immense workload. But the task was still so daunting. They would have to do now in one week, what used to take him eight months to do. He was determined to reach his goal. His wife stirred beside him, and he placed his hand gently on her side. At last he began to relax. He clicked the light off, stared briefly into the darkness, then closed his eyes.

On your mark. . . get set. . . go

At 6:14 AM the alarm rang. Groggily, Tony reached over his slumbering wife and depressed the snooze button. Seven minutes later, the alarm rang out again, and this time Tony swung his legs over the edge of the bed, and propped himself up. He reached up and massaged his eyes vigorously, encouraging them to open, then stumbled to the shower.

Forty-five minutes later Tony was in his car, his nerves sizzling from his first coffee of the morning. Excitement filled him, but so did the anxiety he experienced the night before. He felt the same way a miler must feel the second after the starter pistol explodes. There was no turning back, no starting over. The race had officially begun. Every second that passed counted, and he had to make sure that everything he did from now on, for the rest of week, moved him closer to the $40,000 goal.

At 7:30, Tony bought another coffee at the cafeteria on the main floor of his office building, then took the elevator up three floors and marched through the front doors of Henderson Financial Planning. He was the first one there, but probably wouldn't be for long. Three other people in his office were early starters, and one of them was Gillian. He was anxious for her to arrive so they could get started. But he could use whatever time he had to jump start things. He walked into his private office at the end of the hall, set his briefcase on the credenza behind his desk, placed the Styrofoam cup of coffee on a coaster, and dropped into his swivel chair. He pushed the power button on his desktop computer and sat back while his hard drive hummed to life.

He watched the screen snap on. Dialogue boxes appeared and he clicked enter a few times. A minute later he was staring at a digital version of the Weekly Hotsheet Gillian had showed him on Friday. He read through it quickly, making mental notes to himself, then opened his drawer and took out his Dictaphone. He spent the next few minutes narrating changes and additions to the Hotsheet. After he was finished doing that he looked down and saw a yellow message slip.

The slip was a note he had written to himself early in the afternoon on the previous Friday, reminding him to pay a visit to his uncle who was convalescing in the hospital. It was something he should do before he left for vacation, otherwise he wouldn't be able to see him for another two weeks. A feeling of dread welled up inside him. The visit to his uncle was something he simply could not delegate. He had to do it himself. But the $40,000 week was upon him, and he knew every minute was precious. He felt guilty for even considering canceling, but deep down he knew he should and would go. He loved his uncle, and certainly family came before business. Still, the question remained — where was he going to find the time? He didn't want to have to cancel a major appointment. Panicked, he called up his digital schedule for the week, and quickly scrolled across it. There were some vacancies, but not many. A half hour here and there between appointments. But he would need more than that, probably two hours. There it was. Between 3 and 5 o'clock on Friday afternoon. That would essentially put the end of the week at 3:00 on Friday. Well, he had no choice — he would have to close the $40,000 before visiting his uncle.

After he blocked off the last two hours of the week for his uncle, Gillian knocked on his half-open office door.

"Morning, Tony," she said.

"Hi, Gillian," Tony replied. "By the way, has Isabel arrived yet?"

"Just now. We rode up in the same elevator."

Tony noted the time. 8 o'clock. She was just on time, and he needed her right away. "Gillian, when you're settled, come back here and we can get started."

"Sure," she said, then disappeared down the hall.

Tony pressed Isabel's extension. "Hi, Izzy," he said into the speaker.

"Morning, T." she replied.

"I have some changes to the Hotsheet. We need them for the 9 o'clock meeting."

"No problem. I'll be right there," she said.

Isabel came into his office, picked up the micro-tape cassette and then returned to her workstation down the hall.

A few minutes later, Gillian stepped into Tony's office and settled into a chair. Her expression was grim.

Tony's heart sank. He had only worked with Gillian for a month, but already he had come to recognize that her grim expressions meant something was definitely up.

"What's up?" Tony asked, bracing himself.

"I just checked my e-mail. They're gonna rate Ambrose."

Tony fell back into his seat, shaking his head. Ambrose owned a successful chain of convenience stores and was one of the biggest prospects on this week's agenda. If they didn't close Ambrose, there would be no way to reach the $40,000 goal. He had personally worked on the case for nearly six months. It had been a roller-coaster ride, but Ambrose had recently agreed to go for his medicals. In fact, the Ambrose case was the first thing Tony and Gillian had worked on together, and Tony was certain that she was the reason Ambrose finally budged.

Gillian had managed to impress the irascible Ambrose with her expertise at insuring small business owners. By comparison, Tony was relatively new at the game, only having had his license for a couple of years. Gillian, however, was a veteran. Not only did she have five years in the insurance business, she had another five years as a CA who worked almost exclusively with small business owners. She knew exactly what Ambrose's needs were, what his risk/return relationships were.

The catch to the Ambrose case was that he had had cancer a few years ago. The cancer was local, a small tumor in his throat, and it had been caught early. There had been no recurring symptoms, and his health was otherwise fine. Gillian and Tony had been optimistic that they could get a standard rating for Ambrose and insure him with the same premium as any other healthy 50 year old. However, alarm bells always went off in the underwriting department when they found out an applicant used to have cancer. As Gillian was now explaining to Tony, Jupiter Life Co. wanted to give Ambrose a 30% rating for three years, after which, if there were no more health problems, they would reduce the rate to standard.

"He's gonna flip," Tony was saying.

"I know," Gillian said, staring at the floor.

"I mean, he may take it in the end, but he's gonna want us to shop around for a better rate, which means it won't close this week."

It wasn't even 9 o'clock on Monday morning, and already it looked like the race was over. Tony felt nauseous. His second coffee was burning a hole in his stomach. He had a picture of himself, glumly slumped in his seat on the plane. No way, he said to himself. He was not going to miss his goal. He stood up with determination, and paced his office.

"What about getting Jupiter Life to re-evaluate Ambrose?"

"Not likely. That's how they rate his cancer. I think it was a close call, but they're being careful."

"What about another company? Is there a chance another underwriter might rate him differently?"

"Sure, especially in a case like this. Another company might certainly see it differently."

"Well, that's what we have to do, then," Tony declared.

"But, it's a time issue," Gillian responded. "Even if you could get a company to look at it, you're not going to get a response by the end of the week."

"You mean it's impossible?"

"Well, no. Not impossible, just not very likely. We'd have to push them."

"Then that's what we'll do. I mean that's what *you'll* do. We'll make that one of your urgent priorities for this week."

Gillian nodded. "Tony," she said, "if we're going to stand a chance on this rating thing, I'd better go now and put a call in to Dean Howard, the head underwriter at Neptune Life — they're our best chance. And I'll have to have all the medical information forwarded right away."

"Well, what are you waiting for, Gillian?" Tony exclaimed excitedly, thrilled that there was still hope. "You'll still be able to make the nine o'clock, won't you. We need you."

Gillian looked at her watch, said, "Yeah, I think so," then hurried out of Tony's office.

The 9 o'clock meeting

At 9 o'clock Tony left his office and went down to the boardroom. Isabel was distributing copies of this week's Hotsheet around the table. Philip and Jerry, Tony's junior salespeople, were sitting together at the left side of the table. Marina, one of the customer service representatives sat beside them. On the other side of the boardroom table were Gina, the marketing support person, and Rye, the other service rep. Tony took his seat at the head of the table. In a few minutes, Gillian rushed in and grabbed her seat on Tony's right. Everyone was present now, except for Vera, the receptionist, who was watching the phones.

Tony turned to Isabel, the administrative assistant, and said, "Thanks for updating the Hotsheet on such short notice."

"No problem," she said, smiling.

"Okay, folks," Tony said firmly and with authority, as though he were captain of a warship, "we have a rather exceptional week ahead of ourselves. I'm not sure how many of you are aware, but we now have our first chance to start meeting our target of $2 million in gross revenue. Take a look at this week's projection." Everyone in the room looked down at their Hotsheets. "For the first time ever, our office has the opportunity to close more than $40,000 of business in one week."

There were murmurs of excitement around the room. Everyone knew that if they managed to close the $40,000 they were on their way to a $2-million year.

"But there's no way we're going to close everything," Philip muttered. "Last couple of weeks, our closing rate was below 90%."

"We've done 100% before, and we're going to do it again this week," said Tony.

Gillian interjected, "I think Tony's right. Look, this week we have seven closing appointments, and all of them are due to close."

"Yeah, but hitting seven out of seven is hard to do. Anything could go wrong. All we need is for one case to stall, or collapse. It happens all the time," Philip said.

"Not this week," Gillian stated, rivaling Tony's optimism.

"But what about the Ambrose case?" Isabel asked. She had heard about the rating.

"What's wrong with the Ambrose case?" Philip asked, alarmed. He had helped Tony on the case before Gillian was brought in, and had kept a close eye on it ever since. He knew the Ambrose case was a big one, for him at least, and he wanted it to close desperately. He sold a lot of small cases, with an average commission below $1,000. With a potential commission of $15,000, Ambrose was the biggest case he had ever worked on. Gillian had certainly helped bring it close to the finish line, but there wouldn't have been an Ambrose case at all, if he hadn't assisted Tony in nurturing it month after month.

Philip glared at Isabel, who nodded in Gillian's direction. Philip's gaze snapped toward Gillian. His mouth agape, waiting.

"They want to rate him," Gillian replied.

Philip shook his head in despair, and there were hushed grumblings around the table.

"Gillian's got it under control, Philip," Tony said, then looked at Gillian for a reassuring nod. Gillian shrugged her shoulders doubtfully, as though to say she was doing all she could, but wasn't holding her breath. Obviously she had been putting on a brave face when she told the group every case this week was due to close. Tony swallowed hard, then turned to face the table.

"Okay, let's get down to business. We don't have any time to waste," Tony said, looking down now at the Hotsheet. "Let's go through everything quickly one-by-one. First, Jerry, you're on top of the Kerston case, right? That's at 10:00 this morning. Any problems?"

"No, everything's under control. I just need to pick up the check," Jerry replied confidently.

"Okay, next," Tony continued, "Philip, you've got the Domino case and the Pundar case this afternoon. Any issues."

"Domino called last Thursday. He was hesitating a little. He wants to see another proposal for a joint-last-to-die policy on him and his wife. If he likes it, I think it'll close."

"Have you got the proposal?" Tony asked, with concern. He knew Domino. Domino was an old client of his that he had passed on to Philip to handle. He was one of those clients you had to hand hold all the time — too much work for Tony now, but good practice for Philip. If the numbers weren't great, Domino would balk for sure, and spin the whole case out another month or two, making Philip run around like mad getting new quotes on a daily basis.

"It's on Philip's desk, right now. I just put it there this morning," Gina, the marketing support person, said.

"And how do the numbers look?" Tony asked.

"Actually they look great. It's a great idea for Domino, I think he'll go for it," Gina said, but Tony knew she didn't know how fickle Domino was.

"Well, okay, it's our only shot, I guess," Tony replied.

Philip nodded.

"And what about the Fibonnacci case later in the week?" Tony asked, jumping ahead to Thursday. Fibonnacci was up there with the Ambrose case as one of the biggest, and toughest of the week. He was relying heavily on Marina and Gina to put together a solid package, something Mario Fibonnacci simply couldn't say no to.

"There are still things I'm waiting for from the fund companies," Marina said. "Everything should come in today."

"That'll give me Tuesday and Wednesday to put something together for you to look at, Tony, before you go see Mario," Gina said.

"Are you sure that's enough time?" Tony said, knowing that the Fibonnacci proposal was a lot of work.

"Just enough," Gina said. Tony noticed a hint of worry wrinkle her brow.

"Okay, I hope so," Tony declared.

The people

The 9 o'clock meeting continued for another half an hour. Tony went down the list, through each appointment, making sure everyone knew exactly what to do. At the end of the meeting, Tony went back to his office. As he sat at his desk, waiting for his digital day planner to appear on his screen, he thought about the morning meeting. It felt great to have an army of talented people to work with. Together, as a team, they could accomplish so much. Years ago, when he was a one-man operation, he ran around like a scalded cat, going back and forth between appointments, couriering many of his own packages, sitting on the phone with underwriters and customer service people at the insurance companies, and trying frantically to keep on top of his mounting backlog of telephone messages. Those were crazy days. He worked twelve-hour days most of the time, and for much less money. Now, Henderson Financial Planning was a well-oiled machine. There was somebody for every task. Marina and Rye handled all the customer service calls. Isabel liaised with the insurance companies during the underwriting process, arranging medicals and lording over the inspection reports. Gina prepared all the proposals and dealt with the mutual fund companies. Philip and Jerry handled all the junior cases. Vera dealt with telephone calls, mail and couriers, and Gillian was now Tony's understudy. All Tony had to do was prospect for new clients and go to big-case appointments. Today, he never even filled out an application. Forms were something he had always dreaded, and now they were someone else's problem.

The technology

As Tony sat at his desk, clicking through his day planner, he realized that there was much more to his organization than just his people — there was the technological infrastructure. A few years ago, Tony had decided to invest in his business and had gone high-tech. He remembered purchasing his first computer system for $15,000, and that was back when he was making $60,000 a year. The $15,000 he spent on computers represented 25% of his annual revenue. He didn't even spend that much on his home each year. But he realized that he wasn't just spending money, he was investing in the future growth of his business. He figured that if he put $15,000 in an investment plan, he could hope for a 10 to 12% return. But by putting it in his business, he realized that he could get something more like a 30% return. It made sense. And it had proved to be a wise decision.

As soon as Tony got his first computer system, he began phasing out his cluttered, over-stuffed filing cabinets, in favor of a digital storage system. He was a long way from a paper-less office, but everything was now perfectly organized and easy to access. Whenever he spoke to a client now, Tony could push a few buttons on his computer and pull up their file. All the information was up-to-date. Isabel was careful at inputting all the latest information. Simply by looking at his screen, Tony was able to speak fluently about the client's problem. Tony knew his clients were impressed. Where else were they going to get such service? Isabel also used the client data base to help schedule appointments. She was on top of anything that might trigger an appointment — a policy expiring, a conversion date approaching, a new baby, a 65th birthday. As a result, Tony and the other salespeople were able to provide excellent, timely service. Every time they called on a client, there was a specific reason, a specific need to be met. Tony thought back to the days, when, desperate to make a buck, he would ransack his files at random, searching for a client who might have money to invest. It was haphazard. And Tony knew that many of his clients' needs had gone unnoticed. But not today. Tony figured his nine computers alone were doing the work of more than four extra full-time people.

Tony studied his day planner, and printed out a copy to carry in his breast pocket. Except for the Domino case, all the Monday appointments were fairly routine — check pick-ups really. He didn't expect there to be a problem, and he was hoping for some good news on Ambrose.

At the end of the day on Monday, everyone met again briefly in the boardroom for an update.

"Okay, let's go around the table," Tony said. "Jerry, how did you make out?"

"Kerston closed," he said, triumphantly.

One down, six to go, Tony thought to himself. He turned to Philip. "Pundar?" he asked.

"Got it," Philip replied.

"Great, and Domino?" Tony asked bracing himself.

"Well," Philip began, stuttering, "I think everything's okay."

"Think? You mean it didn't close?" Tony asked.

"Well, he wants you to come see him. He says he's your client. He wants to deal with you on this one," Philip uttered nervously.

"Philip, I have confidence in you. Listen, Domino is your client now. You have to close the case, Philip, not me. There's no way Henderson Financial Planning is going to meet the $2-million mark if I have to go around chasing small clients. You have to earn his trust and confidence." Tony was tempted to go in and save the case, but that wouldn't be wise. He meant it when he told Philip he had confidence in him. That's what Philip and Jerry were there for — to work with the smaller clients. Plus, he didn't want to be Philip's crutch. Domino was just giving him a hard time. He probably enjoyed getting a rise out of Philip. If Henderson Financial Planning was going to reach its weekly target, they were going to do it properly, with everyone doing what they were supposed to be doing. Tony was putting his faith in the practice of delegation. He knew that if he strayed off course, started meddling in other people's roles, the organization could break down. He had to trust his team.

Philip nodded meekly, "Okay."

"You can do it," Tony said comfortingly.

Tony then turned to Gillian. "Any word on Ambrose?"

"No," she replied. "Neptune has the medicals. They were sent off this morning. I spoke to Dean, and told him we were looking for a quick turn-around. He said he'd do everything he could."

They wrapped up their meeting and everyone went home, cautiously optimistic about meeting the goal.

On Tuesday, Tony was busy with appointments, but none of them were closings. He was meeting with a couple of big prospects and hoping to gain their confidence, but getting the sale would be a few weeks down the road. As it turned out, the meetings were very positive and Tony felt good about both cases. When he met with the rest of the office, he discovered that Tuesday had pretty much gone off without a hitch, but there was still no Ambrose news. As for Domino, Philip was meeting with him again on Friday.

On Wednesday, Jerry closed two more cases. Four down, three to go. Domino was still outstanding, so were Ambrose and Fibonnacci. They had a long way to go. The last three cases represented more than 75% of the week's projection. Fibonnacci would probably go smoothly, but Tony was concerned about Philip and Domino, and was extremely worried about Ambrose. Gillian had put three anxious calls in to Dean on Wednesday, but hadn't heard back yet. As for Gina and Marina, they had spent almost the entire day developing a dazzling multimedia presentation for Fibonnacci, complete with sound effects. Gina was a genius with technology and Tony walked into many tense appointments knowing he would be able to blow away his prospects with Gina's high-tech wizardry. When Tony reviewed the presentation, he had only a couple of small changes, otherwise it was perfect.

As expected, the Fibonnacci case closed on Thursday afternoon. Tony breathed a sigh of relief. He could smell the finish line. He was back in the office by 2:30, and when he ran into Gillian in the hall, he saw her smile, cautiously.

"Ambrose?" he asked.

"You better rub your lucky rabbit's foot," she said. "Dean says there's a good chance it'll go through by noon tomorrow. No promises."

"What's the hold up?"

"He says their medical officer is taking another look at it, just to make sure."

"Is there any thing else you can do?" he asked, knowing there wasn't.

"No. We wait, and we pray." Gillian swiveled on her heel, in the direction of her office, then spun back again toward Tony. "Oh, Fibonnacci?" She asked.

"Done," Tony replied, pointing his index finger in the air, and blowing over it, like it was a smoking gun.

"So, we're almost there?"

"Almost."

"Well, if Ambrose goes, that leaves Domino," Gillian exclaimed with noticeable excitement.

Tony sighed, and shrugged his shoulders. He didn't really want to think about how the whole week might hang on Philip and Domino.

It was Friday afternoon. Tony ran down to the cafeteria on the main floor and ordered a sandwich. He was flipping nervously through the newspaper, waiting for his order. Dean hadn't yet called Gillian back, but he was going to any second now. A few minutes later, Tony's tuna salad on brown was ready, but he had lost his appetite. He took one look at it and asked the man behind the counter if he could have it to go instead.

As he stepped back into his office, he heard Gillian let out a yelp of excitement. She came bounding around the corner. "We got Ambrose. They approved him two minutes ago. I got Ambrose on the phone right after that. I'm heading over there right now to pick up a check for the first annual premium."

"Was Ambrose excited?" Tony asked.

"He couldn't help but be excited. I had enough for both of us."

"Excellent job," Tony said, extending a hand out to her.

"Thanks," she said, "I couldn't have done it without you." She laughed then disappeared out the door.

"Any word from Philip?" Tony asked Vera.

"No," she replied, "he's still out with Domino. I don't think he'll be back until 2:30."

It was coming right down to the wire. At 3:00 Tony would have to leave to visit his uncle.

At about twenty minutes after two, Tony assembled everyone in the boardroom — everyone except Vera who was still watching the phones, and, of course, Philip.

"I hope nobody has anything pressing to get to before Monday," said Tony, "because if not, you can start enjoying your weekend pretty soon."

"Did we make the target?" Jerry asked, assuming that's why Tony called everyone into the boardroom.

"Not yet. We still don't know about Domino."

Everyone exchanged glances. Anticipation hung in the room. At the center of the table was a bottle of champagne, still corked, and a circle of upturned glasses. If Philip came back with good news, the bottle would be uncorked. If not, it would go back into the fridge.

The seconds ticked away on the boardroom clock, slowly, agonizingly. There was occasional chatter, but mostly, everyone was quiet. Tony leaned back in his chair, drumming his fingers on the oak tabletop. 2:30 came and went, and still no sign of Philip.

Gillian looked at Tony. She raised her eyebrows. "He's probably not coming back, you know. He's drowning his sorrows at some bar, because he didn't get it." She said it with some jest, but there was an undercurrent of vexation.

"Yeah, Tony, I think you should have taken the Domino case," Jerry said. "I mean, if this week means so much to us."

"That's exactly why I didn't take this case. The revenue is one matter, but we all have to be able to rely on each other, and have confidence in each other's abilities. If Philip doesn't close the Domino case, we have to assume that I wouldn't have been able to either."

"But that's hardly true," Jerry snorted.

"How do you know?" Tony returned. "Domino's unpredictable. Nothing's a sure thing with him. I remember numerous closings I had with him that never closed. He's like that. The point is, he's Philip's client. Not mine. It would be different if there was some need for my expertise, but there isn't. Philip has all the talent and skill he needs to close Domino."

It was getting close to 3:00, and Tony would have to leave soon.

The bottle lay dormant at the center of the table. Everyone was looking at it sadly, preparing to send it back where it came from.

Suddenly, Tony heard the front door to the office open. A few seconds later, Philip popped his head through the doorway to the boardroom.

"You guys waiting for me?"

"No," Isabel said jokingly. "What gives you that idea."

"Have a seat, Philip," Tony said.

Philip walked around the table, pulled out a chair, and slipped into it. He put both his hands on the table, and bowed his head.

In defeat, Gillian exhaled a breath of air. It was over. Philip didn't get it, she could tell.

"Well, Philip?" Tony asked haltingly.

Philip raised his head, and scanned the anxious faces around the table. "He didn't go for the last-to-die," he said, with a shake of his head.

Jerry gasped audibly.

Then Philip spoke up again, "Gina had put together another proposal, a variation on something we showed him a month ago. The new one showed guaranteed premiums for ten years. After that the policy is paid-up for life."

Everyone leaned closer to the table, wondering where Philip was going.

"Domino decided to take that instead." Philip was grinning.

Tony fell back in his chair. They had done it. Then panic seized him. "Hey, Philip," he asked, "what's the commission on that?"

"Enough. More than enough."

Tony jumped up and reached for the bottle. He popped the cork. They were on their way to a $2-million year.

In fact, Tony did $2.5 million that year. And revenues have continued to grow ever since at a dramatic pace. Today, Tony has over a dozen employees in his organization, and fourteen computers.

Tony's business grew so dramatically because he utilized the seventh best practice — delegate. Let's briefly review those strategies and how Tony used them.

Strategy 1: Delegate to other people

When I first met Tony seven years before the events of this story took place, he worked almost completely alone. He received some assistance from a shared receptionist, but for all intents and purposes, he was a one-man operation. He had the makings of a great salesman, but because he did most of his own administrative work, and all of his own customer service work, he had relatively little time to practice his salesmanship. When we originally talked about his plans for the future, it was clear to me that Tony wanted to grow his business not just make sales. Tony began to see his career in a different light. He would no longer be a salesman who made his living from a commission income, he would be an entrepreneur who owned a financial planning company. It was a big conceptual shift for Tony. Immediately, he could see the implications. Instead of taking his commission income and looking for other investments, he saw the merit in plowing his income back into the business, growing it. Investing in himself — in his business — was his best investment. Not long after we first met, Tony hired a part-time administrative assistant. Later that same year, she went full-time. Tony didn't have to wait long to see the benefit of delegating work to his assistant. The more he unloaded onto her, the more time he had to do what he did best — develop relationships with prospects and clients. His sales took off. He made more than enough money to pay his assistant's salary. The return on his investment was over 30% — he didn't know many investment opportunities that could rival that.

Over the years, Tony plowed more and more of his earnings back into hiring additional people. Each new hire performed a specialized task in his business, from customer service to marketing support. And with each hire, Tony had more time to concentrate solely on developing relationships with clients and prospects.

As Tony expanded his operation, he learned the value of creating an environment that attracted new and talented people. Without the right people, Tony's practice of delegation would fail. Gillian was a real coup for Tony. She had heard good things about Henderson Financial Planning from a friend, and when she came to visit the office for her first interview, she was excited to see a highly developed, computerized environment. She knew that this was the kind of company she could help grow. Gillian, in fact, turned out to be one of Tony's most important assets. As an insurance expert she was able to work on cases of a complexity Tony would never have been able to handle. She was largely responsible for taking the company to it's $2.5-million mark during her first year. And for that, she was well rewarded. Tony needed her, and let her know that loud and clear when it came time to hand out the Christmas bonuses.

Strategy 2: Delegate to technology

Tony did more than just delegate to people; he delegated to technology — specifically computers. As we saw in the story, Tony made an aggressive, but wise, investment of $15,000 in computer equipment seven years earlier. Tony realized that he didn't have to spend hours each week trying to organize and keep track of his files, he could delegate a large portion of that activity to a computer. Hiring an assistant gave Tony more time to spend with his clients and prospects, but so did the new computer. Over the years, Tony continued to invest in the latest computer technology, eventually reaching the point where today he estimates that his 14 computers are doing the work of seven extra people.

Today, Tony also uses technology to create client capital. His computers store, retrieve and analyze useful information about clients and prospects. His team uses this computer power to anticipate and respond to their clients' needs, wants and values.

In the first two months of this year, Henderson Financial Planning processed over 1,500 contributions to retirement plans. The company's client management system had identified eligible clients and prepared letters. An automatic dialing feature had allowed staff to call for appointments, and book every minute of the salespeople's time. This combination of high-tech and high-touch increases client loyalty.

Strategy 3: Build an organization

The last strategy for delegation is build an organization. Tony hired people and purchased computer equipment, but he also realized that it was crucial to organize the people and the computers in such a way that the process of delegation was efficient. As Tony grew his business, he developed and redeveloped a reliable process for handling every aspect of his company. There was a process for everything. Tony knew exactly what was required to build his sales. He was the business developer, whose main roles were working with the big clients and prospecting. Whenever he went out on cases, he brought Gillian along with him. She was in charge of any background work that needed to be done, such as research and developing presentations. And for the presentations, she would work closely with Gina, the marketing support person. Philip and Jerry handled all the small clients. Isabel was there to oversee the underwriting process, and Marina and Rye provided customer service. Vera, who ran the reception desk, knew exactly where every single call should be routed. With every new hire, Tony re-jigged the process of delegation. Henderson Financial Planning was a complex weave of interdependent roles, and it was greater, much greater than its parts. With the whole of Henderson Financial Planning to depend on, Tony was able to reach the stratosphere in sales. Today, Tony's take-home income is in the seven-figure range, something he could never have done on his own.

Best Practice Number 7: Delegate

1) Delegate to other people.
2) Delegate to technology.
3) Build an organization.

These were the people
who went to the charity balls,
the big fund-raisers, who lived
in three-car-garage homes
and had limousine drivers.
Her knees went weak.
The opportunity in the auditorium
was bigger than anything
she had come across before. . . .
She thanked herself for having
the foresight to bring
Peter and Henry along.

Chapter 10

Best Practice Number 8: Utilize resources

I n the last chapter, we saw how you can use the seventh best practice — delegate — to free you up so you can spend more of your time developing relationships with your clients and prospects. In this chapter, we'll explore how you can use the eighth best practice — utilize resources — to make better use of your time and further enrich those relationships.

We'll look at five strategies for utilizing resources: 1) Use information sources. 2) Hire consultants to develop your infrastructure. 3) Work with your suppliers. 4) Develop mentoring relationships. 5) Work with collateral professionals. I'd like to begin our exploration of these strategies by telling you another story from Rebecca's career.

Star chamber

Rebecca's heels clicked rhythmically on the old hardwood floor. She and a man named Peter Fowler were marching down the narrow hallway of a sprawling, turn-of-the-century home on a peaceful street just east of the hectic downtown core. A few feet ahead, to her right, was a large, ornately-framed oil painting. It was a portrait of an elderly man. That must be Stuart Francis, Rebecca thought. Stuart had been a shrewd, wealthy industrialist. During his lifetime he was known to be a miser, but when he died he left a ton of money to start a foundation for disabled children. It had been a surprise to the community, but it was soon discovered that, two months before his death, his first grandson had been born with cerebral palsy. The mansion become the foundation's headquarters. As Rebecca passed the painting she looked into Stuart's eyes, and felt his penetrating stare. It sent an eerie shiver down her spine. His presence was still so strong in the house. It unsettled her more than it would have normally, she thought, because today she was on edge to begin with.

It was a big day for her. The task ahead was not a simple one. And it was something she knew she would not be able to accomplish alone. That's why Peter Fowler was here. He was her trump card. Peter was a short, older man in his 50s. He had been in the insurance business for over 25 years and was now fairly well-known as a writer for many of the industry journals and as a speaker. She actually felt a little star-struck walking beside him.

Meeting your mentor

Rebecca had first met Fowler a few months ago at an insurance conference on the topic of charitable giving. He was the keynote speaker, and Rebecca had been impressed with his speech. The speaker before Fowler had been one of those hyperactive motivational speakers, bouncing around the stage like a gibbon. Fowler was such a contrast. He took to the podium with slow, mincing steps, changing the entire pace of the conference, even before he uttered a word. Rebecca could feel the shift in the crowd, like everyone was suddenly coming down from a high. Maybe the contrast would be too much. Rebecca sensed that everyone was anticipating another spectacle. But if that's what they were waiting for, they were going to be in for a big surprise. When Fowler finally arrived at the lectern, he reached out, pulled the mike toward him and began his speech, in a near whisper. The entire audience leaned forward. He had their attention, but not the way they might have expected — no loud exclamations, no thunderous roars — just the soft voice of a highly intelligent mind. Fowler continued to speak that way for almost an hour. It was riveting in its simplicity. He barely moved an inch. There was the occasional flourish with his hands to emphasize a point, but that was it. There was no need for theater; the content was brilliant. He spoke about how to market charitable giving packages, how to approach foundations and charities and sell them on the idea of raising money through insurance packages. He delved into the complexities of tax law, accounting procedures, revenue projections, the incredible benefits to the charities, to the givers. It was an area of the business Rebecca had never dealt with, but it was certainly an exciting market, and by the end of Fowler's speech she had, in fact, decided to make it her next market.

As everyone was filing out of the auditorium, Rebecca noticed a small throng of people surrounding Fowler at the edge of the stage. She could see that they were members of the audience thanking and congratulating him. As she watched them exchange handshakes with Fowler, an idea flashed in her mind. She was suddenly filled with excitement. She made her way toward Fowler, but waited until the crowd dispersed, leaving Fowler to pack his things.

When she approached him he was bent over his briefcase, shuffling his papers inside.

"Excuse me, Mr. Fowler," she said.

Mr. Fowler stood up, and smiled at her. "Hello," he said.

"My name is Rebecca Hoyle. That was a great speech."

"Thank you," he answered.

"I was wondering whether or not you ever work with other agents on charitable-giving cases."

"Certainly," he answered, "I do a lot of joint work these days."

"Would you mind if I called you in on a case?" Rebecca asked.

"Not at all. Why don't you give me a ring when I'm at the office and we can talk more about it. I'm always interested in working with younger agents." He handed her his card.

They shook hands and Rebecca, thrilled about the prospect of a new market, left the auditorium and returned to her office. She had an important call to make.

The wise man's wisdom

As she continued down the hall with Mr. Fowler, Rebecca thought back to the call she had made after hearing him speak. It was to an old friend of hers, Joan Rider, who was on the board of Francis House. Rebecca briefly explained the concept, and then suggested that Joan should let her make a presentation to a group of potential donors to the charity. Joan seemed interested, but said she would need to get the board members to approve the concept first. She asked Rebecca to send her more information to get things started, and said she would bring it up at their next meeting later in the month.

About six weeks later, Joan finally called back to say the board members were interested, but still needed more information before supporting the concept. Rebecca enlisted Peter Fowler's help, and together they met with Joan and key members of the charity. After a series of meetings that took place over a two-month period the board said they liked the idea, but expressed concern about legal and taxation issues. To answer those concerns, Rebecca enlisted the help of Jeff, a tax lawyer she knew. She organized a meeting between the board and Jeff, and gave them the chance to barrage him with questions. They asked a number of questions that raised complex issues, but Jeff was able to assure them that everything was proper. At last, the board came down to its final concern — finding potential donors willing to make donations through insurance on their lives. Rebecca and Peter said they would be playing a big role in marketing the idea and getting the enrollments. All they needed was the charity's support. Finally, they got the approval they needed.

Rebecca and Peter Fowler met right away to discuss how they would go about conducting a seminar for a group of potential donors for the charity.

"We'll need a full multi-media presentation," Fowler suggested.

"Really?" Rebecca asked, surprised to hear that coming from the man who delivered a one-hour presentation without any technological support, save a microphone.

"It works well in front of potential donors. An all-out show is impressive, instills confidence."

"Do you have a presentation like that ready?" Rebecca asked.

"Me?" Fowler laughed heartily into the phone. "I don't know the first thing about stuff like that. I can barely figure out how to use my speaker phone."

"Well, then?" Rebecca asked, puzzled. "What are we going to do?"

"A few of the insurance companies I deal with have excellent presentations. They even supply the equipment. Recently, I've been using Neptune Life. They have a guy there named Henry Gross who does the actual presenting — he's very good."

"Oh," Rebecca said, "that sounds like a good idea. I'd never thought about getting someone else to do the presentation for us."

"Why not?" Fowler asked. "Look, I can sell. But when it comes to these light shows, I'm a fish out of water. Gross is an amazing presenter, but he can't sell — doesn't want to. I let him do what he does best, and he let's me do what I do best. Plus, he makes me look smart."

"Gotcha," Rebecca said, absorbing the wisdom from a wise man.

Rebecca and Peter Fowler came to the end of the hallway. They were standing in front of a thick wooden door, with a pebbled glass window. A brass plaque beside the door frame said 'Office of the Foundation.' Rebecca pressed a small red buzzer. A bell rang gratingly, and Rebecca heard the shuffle of footsteps beyond the door.

The door opened, and Joan greeted Rebecca.

"Hi, Becky, how are you?" Joan asked.

"Great, Joan, you?"

"Fine. A little swamped though, trying to get things ready for tonight's meeting."

"Hi," said Joan, reaching to shake Peter's hand. "Nice to see you again."

"And *you*," Peter said charmingly. "I'd like to thank you again for giving us this opportunity. We're really excited about the things we can do for the charity."

Joan ushered them into her office.

Peter continued, "We just did a group of twenty donors for the Bedrich Institute that will raise over $50 million for them."

Joan nodded, impressed. "Well, I'd sure like you to do the same for us. It would make my job a lot easier."

Joan showed Rebecca and Peter a couple of chairs in the corner of her office. "Do you mind waiting here? We've got fifteen minutes before everyone arrives, and there are a few things I still have to do."

"Not at all," Peter said.

Joan walked over to her desk. "There's someone else coming, isn't there?"

"Yes, a Mr. Gross will be arriving any minute now."

"Great," Joan said as she sat at her desk and began to type frantically on her computer.

Rebecca and Peter chatted quietly in the corner, careful not to disrupt Joan. A few minutes later, the buzzer went. Joan's head snapped up in surprise. The bell had obviously jolted her out of deep concentration.

"Must be Henry," Rebecca said. "I'll get it," she offered.

Joan nodded and quickly returned to her computer.

"Hi, Henry," Peter said as Rebecca lead Henry toward their corner.

Henry was a tall, thin man. Somewhere in his late 30s, Rebecca figured. He had prematurely white, thinning hair, and a narrow, but kind-looking face. It was the round, close-set eyes that gave him a gentle appearance. He was carting two large cases, and he set them down cautiously on the floor beside himself.

"Great to see you again, Peter," Henry said, then glanced toward Joan at the desk.

"They'll be with us in a minute," Rebecca said, gesturing for Henry to take a seat.

Ten minutes later, Joan let out a deep sigh, and leaned back in her chair, looking over at Rebecca.

"Finito!" She exclaimed, then, addressing everyone in the corner, "Why don't we head downstairs and get ready."

Rebecca, Peter and Henry stood up and followed Joan through the door, into the hall, and down a set of winding stairs at the back of the house. In the basement, Joan led them through two brass-knobbed doors into an auditorium. Henry lugged his two cases over to a table near the stage, then unpacked his multimedia equipment, which consisted of a slide projector, and a portable stereo system. Peter and Rebecca sat down in the two chairs next to the table.

A few minutes later, people started to arrive and Joan greeted them at the door. Quickly, the room filled with older men and women, a good representation of the city's affluent. These were the people who went to the charity balls, the big fund-raisers, who lived in three-car-garage homes and had limousine drivers. Her knees went weak. The opportunity in the auditorium was bigger than anything she had come across before. She saw Peter wave to someone he recognized in the audience. Rebecca smiled to herself;

she knew how valuable that recognition was. She thanked herself for having the foresight to bring Peter and Henry along.

There were now thirty or so people in the room. Joan approached Rebecca and said, "Looks like we're ready. You're first on the agenda. So, I'll get things started."

Joan walked to the rostrum, and said over the microphone, "Today we are pleased to have with us Rebecca Hoyle. She and her team are going to spend the next hour showing us a very innovative method of raising money for Francis House." She turned away from the rostrum and held out her hand, inviting Rebecca to take the stage.

A surge of adrenaline exploded inside Rebecca, and she found her breath catching in her throat. She took a few seconds to breathe nice and slowly, then felt herself relax. She walked over to the wooden rostrum and leaned into the mike. "Thank you very much, Joan. We truly appreciate the opportunity to show Francis House how they can raise money by taking advantage of the preferred tax status of insurance vehicles. For the next half hour my colleague from Neptune Life, Henry Gross, is going to give us a presentation. Afterwards, Peter Fowler, an expert on using insurance to fund charities, is going to say a few words, then we'll open it up to questions. Thank you."

Rebecca waited while Henry approached the rostrum, then moved to take her seat again. She was light-headed, but felt she had spoken clearly and confidently. For the next little while she could sit back and relax.

Over the following half hour, Henry took the audience through his dazzling presentation. As he spoke he flipped through slides that clearly outlined the issues and benefits of funding a charity through insurance. Staggering amounts of money could be raised by relatively small premiums. Rebecca sensed that the crowd was extremely interested.

Henry finished. It was Peter's turn. Again, it was like time slowed down, while he minced toward the podium. At the microphone, he cocked his head forward, gazed out over the wooden ledge of the lectern, and scanned the audience. His eyes cast a spell of rapture. It was incredible to see this amazing effect all over again, and this time with a group of wealthy prospects. It was no wonder Peter Fowler was a top salesman. When he was finished, Rebecca could see that people were eager to ask questions.

Over the next little while, Peter took questions from the audience. For some of the questions, he deferred to Henry, who was able to give expert answers. Rebecca was thrilled. She was part of a team, a wonderful team. Together, she, Peter and Henry were going to do some great business.

When all the questions were answered and it came time to leave, a number of people got up from their seats and approached Peter. One person, a white-haired gentleman with gold rimmed glasses, told Peter he was very impressed and said he would seriously consider making a donation via an insurance policy on his life. "What I like about it is the long-term perspective," he said. "Charities like Francis always seem to be running around trying to raise the money to survive from month to month. But that's dangerous. I want this charity to have a future. I want to make sure Francis House is around in twenty years, not just next week. And I want to do my part."

"I'm glad to hear you say that," Peter replied to the man in his charming manner. "I'd like to get a group of people who think the same way you do, and put an entire package together."

"I'll help you get those people," the man said, handing Peter his card. "Call me first thing in the morning. I already know who I'm going to call on this thing."

They shook hands and the man departed.

Rebecca, Peter and Henry left the Francis mansion and stood outside in the parking lot for a quick debrief, before getting into their cars.

"I think we've got a live one here," Peter said. "I can usually tell when someone's serious about the idea or not. That one gentleman back there was very serious. You could see it in his eyes. Some people don't always mean what they say, but that man did. I think this Francis House thing will work out. Good work, Rebecca." He shook her hand firmly.

Rebecca was nearly overcome with excitement. She was the one who arranged the presentation, but clearly Peter and Henry were the ones who sold it. And she would be splitting 50/50 whatever business came from it with Peter. And Henry's company would underwrite it all. She, of course, would be responsible for doing a lot of the legwork; she knew Peter didn't get too involved in the nitty-gritty of insurance applications or the arranging of medicals, but Rebecca was more than happy to take over that role. She'd be delegating most of it, anyway.

In the twelve months that followed their initial presentation to Francis House, Rebecca and Peter managed to place a total of $20 million of coverage on 14 lives — and there was still more business to come.

Throughout the Francis case, Rebecca made use of the five strategies for utilizing resources. Some of the strategies had a more direct impact than others, but all of them played a role in the ultimate success of the case. Let's go behind the scenes and take a closer look at how Rebecca was able to apply the five strategies.

Strategy 1: Use information sources

Rebecca knew that the success of her presentation depended on having the right type of people at the event. In particular she wanted people who were familiar with Francis House and who were known to be wealthy, generous donors. Many of these people were probably not aware of the power of insurance as a fund-raising vehicle. If she could expose the idea to them, she would surely get their attention. She knew Joan would be promoting the event through her newsletter and possibly a flyer to her regular mailing list, but Rebecca was concerned that wouldn't be enough. She wanted to make sure the big players came. She asked Joan if she had an exclusive list of their top donors. Joan said she did. Rebecca then offered to put together a more elegant promotional package and invitation just for the people on that list, and send it out on a special mailing. Joan thought that was a great idea, so long as it was at Rebecca's expense, and so long as Joan mailed out the packages herself — the mailing list was confidential.

When Rebecca first caught a glimpse of the crowd that night at Francis House, she knew her utilization of the Francis House mailing list had paid off.

Throughout her career, Rebecca has learned the value of seeking out information sources to help grow her business. She is constantly on the lookout for mailing lists, such as the exclusive one for Francis House, and listings of local businesses. She subscribes to and reads a number of trade magazines for the various industries she target markets, and uses the library and the internet often as way of developing and researching leads.

Strategy 2: Hire consultants to develop your infrastructure

When it came time to put together the invitation and the promo package for the Francis House donors, Rebecca asked Omar, a computer consultant she used from time to time, to come in and demonstrate to Irma, her administrative assistant, how to use their new desktop publishing program. Rebecca wanted more than just a regular promo package; she wanted to really impress the Francis House donors. She didn't want it to be something they could just ignore or throw away; she wanted their attention and she wanted to make certain they came on the night of the presentation. Omar spent a total of six hours over three days training Irma on the publishing program. After he left, Irma was practically an expert, and the package she eventually produced for Rebecca was superb. Rebecca knew that it always paid to ask the experts. If she left Irma to struggle with the new program, Irma would have wasted valuable time and certainly would not have produced as impressive a package.

Over the years Rebecca has used a number of outside resources to help her infrastructure run more efficiently. For instance, she has called on other computer specialists to set up an internal network for her office, bookkeepers to come in and help with the accounting, and even a massage therapist to come in once in a while to help reduce the stress levels of her and her employees.

Strategy 3: Work with your suppliers

One of the most valuable things Rebecca learned from working with Peter was the strategy of utilizing her suppliers as a resource. Henry

Gross was a marketing support person at Neptune Life and it was his job to go around and make presentations on behalf of brokers. As part of a large company, Gross had access to lots of equipment, and had the ability to arrange a rather impressive seminar. By utilizing Gross, Rebecca was able to borrow the prestige and expertise of Neptune Life.

Since the Francis House case, Rebecca continued to utilize Gross as a resource. But she also learned to take advantage of some of her suppliers' other resources, such as their actuaries and investment specialists. Rebecca no longer felt the pressure to master everything herself. She was able to expand the breadth and depth of the services she offered to her clients simply by borrowing the expertise from her suppliers.

Rebecca has also taken advantage of the marketing budgets of her supplier companies. Recently, she did the same thing my client Tony used to do; she purchased advertising time on a local radio show, ran 60-second spots advertising her services, and had Neptune Life subsidize half the cost of the ads.

Strategy 4: Develop mentoring relationships

Finding Peter Fowler was nothing short of a watershed moment in Rebecca's career. With Peter as her colleague she was able to close cases of a complexity and caliber that she could not have done on her own. Not only did she see the immediate rise in her income, but she also benefited from watching a master at work, and learning from his wisdom.

Rebecca has continued to work with Peter Fowler, and the relationship is certainly beneficial to both. Through Rebecca, Peter realizes opportunities he otherwise would not have. Without Rebecca, there would have been no Francis House case. Plus, Peter Fowler benefits emotionally from the sheer enjoyment of passing on his wisdom to a young and eager student.

It is important to remember that we choose our mentors; they don't choose us. You can't wait for a mentor to come along; you have go out and actively search for one.

Strategy 5: Work with collateral professionals

Another resource that played a key role in the Francis House case was the tax lawyer, Jeff. Instead of trying to wrestle with the legal issues herself, something Rebecca was clearly not qualified to do, she sought the help of an expert. The board members had confidence in Jeff's answers because he was a respected specialist in his field. Had Rebecca tried to do the case without turning to Jeff as a resource, she probably would not have been able to get the board to approve the concept.

Aside from Jeff, Rebecca has used many other collateral professionals as resources. As a financial planner who often steps into complicated cases, Rebecca is constantly bringing in corporate lawyers, accountants and other investment advisors.

Through the use of the above five strategies, Rebecca has been able to enrich the service she provides to her prospects and clients. The service she offers is much greater than the service she used to offer when she worked primarily alone, and today her clients have come to rely on her as a conduit to a broad range of expertise.

Best Practice Number 8: Utilize Resources

1) Use information sources.
2) Hire consultants to develop your infrastructure.
3) Work with your suppliers.
4) Develop mentoring relationships.
5) Work with collateral professionals.

When I first met him
nine years ago he was working
frantically, and earning
$60,000 a year. Minutes ago,
he had just finished telling me
that Henderson Financial Planning
had grossed over $3 million so far,
and it was only June.

Chapter 11

Beyond the 8 Best Practices

Throughout this book we have explored what the 8 Best Practices are and how you can use them to become a high-performing salesperson. But the 8 Best Practices are much more than that. They are a way of transforming yourself from a top salesperson into a successful business owner. I'd like to end this book by showing you how you can use the 8 Best Practices to take your business through the three stages all successful businesses must go through: 1) Finding qualified prospects. 2) Finding time. 3) Business continuation.

Let's explore how Tony used the power of the 8 Best Practices to grow his business.

Stage 1: Finding qualified prospects

The first six best practices are really about taking your business through stage one. In this stage your primary concern is finding enough prospects to turn into clients in order to earn a living. You are doing everything you can to keep the pipeline that fuels your business full.

When I first met Tony, he was in stage one. He was run ragged, chasing an endless string of prospects, trying to increase his sales. When he changed his behavior and used best practice number one — develop and utilize a marketing plan — he was really practicing a more efficient way of identifying and developing prospects.

When Tony began to utilize best practice number 2 — know your client — he was able to begin the process of turning those prospects into clients because he understood their personal and business needs. To move one step closer to the sale he then had to use best practice number 3 — understand how people make decisions. Applying that practice meant knowing what it would take to motivate each individual client to make the buying decision. Finally, he was able to close sales using the fourth best practice — help your prospects and clients to buy.

Next, in order to make the most of every single prospect, Tony realized he had to readjust the way he looked at his relationships with his clients. Instead of focusing on single sales, Tony began creating client capital so he could harvest his clients, and provide continuous service, selling to them as new needs arose.

In order to prevent the pipeline from drying up, Tony began using best practice number 6 — obtain introductions. Tony found that he could generate a wealth of excellent prospects and close a high percentage of them by hitchhiking on the credibility of his existing client base. As a result of his skill at obtaining introductions, his business exploded.

Unfortunately, after making full use of the first six practices, Tony's pipeline was so full, he simply couldn't provide the same high level of service to all his prospects and clients — there wasn't enough time.

Whereas, only months earlier *prospects* had been Tony's most precious resource and the source of his wealth, suddenly *time* became his most valuable commodity. He was experiencing the same problem that all high-performing salespeople encounter at some point in their careers. He had run out of time and thus entered stage two of the business development cycle.

Stage 2: Finding time

In order to find the time to take his business to the next level, Tony turned to best practices 7 and 8. When Tony began to fully utilize best practice number 7 — delegate — he was able to develop an organization around him that allowed him to focus his energies on what he does best — develop relationships with prospects and clients. As a result, his business became even more profitable, even though he was spending significant amounts of money on employees and technology. Tony's company was beginning to look a lot like a serious business.

As his business continued to expand, Tony then started focusing on best practice number 8. He had always used this practice to some extent, but he now turned it on full force. Delegation gave him more free time. He spent that time cultivating and utilizing outside resources to open new markets and help him close cases — ultimately enriching his relationships with his prospects and clients.

However, the success of these last two best practices actually brought Tony up against another limit to his growth. Although he was more successful than ever, his business had one problem — Tony. Henderson Financial Planning's flaw was that it was dependent on Tony's ability to work. Without Tony, the business would suffer dearly. He now found himself on the brink of the third stage of the business development cycle.

Stage 3: Business continuation

Business continuation allows you to capitalize on your years of hard work. After spending what may be decades growing your business, you will eventually want to relax and reap the rewards of your lifelong investment. Either you will want to sell your stake in your business or retire and continue to draw on its profits as it operates without you. Either way, you don't want it to collapse the minute you step away. In order to prevent that, you will have to develop your business so that it can thrive without you. This brings you to stage three — business continuation.

Succession planning

In order to break through the last limit of the business cycle, you will need to begin disengaging yourself from your company. To do this, you will have to extend best practices 7 and 8 as far as you can. You will have to find another person or other people who can do exactly what you do, as well as you do, or, hopefully, even better. Tony was able to find Gillian, the CA with top-notch insurance skills, and begin grooming her to be his successor when he retires.

Today, Tony is still in the process of completing stage three, but he is well on his way.

Tony's succession plan

As part of Tony's succession plan, he makes a point of taking Gillian along with him on all his sales calls. By bringing her to his clients and telling them how much he trusts her and what her qualifications are, he is transferring his clients' loyalty from him to Gillian. When he leaves for his early retirement, he wants Gillian to be able to step into his role without Henderson Financial Planning losing a single client.

Tony makes the effort to transfer client loyalty not just to Gillian, but to Henderson Financial Planning as a whole. A good example of this is how he handled Philip and the Domino case. If you remember, during that first, all-important $40,000 week, Tony refused to break down and visit his cranky client, Mr. Domino, even though Philip was worried he might lose the case. Domino had even insisted on seeing Tony, but still he refused to take over Philip's responsibility. He knew how important it was to have confidence in Philip and to encourage his clients to develop relationships with his employees instead of him.

Managing risk in your business

Business continuation is all about managing risk. Whether you are putting a succession plan into action, or developing your client's loyalty to the business, you are always trying to protect against a potential loss. You must now follow the same advice you give to your clients when you tell them how important it is to invest outside their businesses. Tony, for example, sees himself as a business owner just like Ivan Kapeck, the man we met in chapter 1. As such, he manages the risks of his business by creating personal assets outside Henderson Financial Planning.

Tony now looks forward to the day when he can leave Henderson Financial Planning, probably by selling it to Gillian, and living off both the gain on his business and his personal investments.

I'd like to end this book with one final, inspirational story.

Fantastic results

A few months ago I attended a charity banquet. There must have been five hundred people in black evening wear already seated in the main ballroom when I arrived. I was winding my way through the linen-covered tables with my wife, Wendy, when suddenly I heard my name being called from the front of the auditorium. When I looked over I saw Tony waving at me from one of the tables. I hadn't seen him in months.

I went over to say hello and we chatted for a few minutes before the event began. I was amazed at what he told me in those few minutes. When the master of ceremonies took the stage, Wendy and I said good-bye to Tony, congratulating him on the good news he had delivered.

After we took our seats back at our table, I couldn't stop thinking about Tony. When I first met him nine years ago he was working frantically, and earning $60,000 a year. Minutes ago, he had just finished telling me that Henderson Financial Planning had grossed over $3 million so far, and it was only June. The year wasn't even half over. More than that, Tony had already taken seven weeks vacation. Clearly his business was beginning to thrive without him. He would soon graduate from stage three of the business cycle. His is truly an incredible story. I shook my head thinking about it. The contrast between the old Tony and the one I had just talked to was startling. He had totally transformed his life. But the amazing thing about Tony is that he is by no means a rare case. I know so many more like him. He is only one of the scores of salespeople who have started to lead fascinating, enriched lives by using the 8 Best Practices.

Moving forward with the 8 best practices

If you are not already a high-performing salesperson, you — like Tony and Rebecca and Alvin — will be able to vault to the highest echelons of the sales profession by changing your behavior and harnessing the power of the 8 Best Practices of high-performing salespeople.

Enjoy the journey.

Beyond the 8 Best Practices

1) Finding qualified prospects.
2) Finding time.
3) Business continuation.

THE 8 BEST PRACTICES OF HIGH-PERFORMING SALESPEOPLE

Best Practice Number 1:
Develop and Utilize a Marketing Plan

Best Practice Number 2:
Know Your Client

Best Practice Number 3:
Understand How People Make Decisions

Best Practice Number 4:
Help Your Prospects and Clients Buy

Best Practice Number 5:
Create Client Capital

Best Practice Number 6:
Obtain Introductions

Best Practice Number 7:
Delegate

Best Practice Number 8:
Utilize Resources

LOOK FOR DAVID COWPER'S
BEST-SELLING BUSINESS BOOK
BREAKTHROUGH

Previewed here:

I passed the turnoff for the highway and slowed down, easing my car onto the shoulder, the tires crunching gravel. It was 6:45 AM and the traffic was light, but steady – brief intervals of silence punctuated by the occasional rush of a car roaring past. I hadn't had much sleep, but my nerves kept me awake. Fifteen minutes to go, and as the seconds ticked away my heart rate accelerated. I needed to relax; everything would depend on my ability to stay focused, controlled. At 7:15 it would all be over. There were two possible results: I would either realize my dream, or it would vanish. Either way, my life would be forever changed.

I looked ahead through the windshield, my eyes following the lines of the highway to the vanishing point, where I fixed my gaze. Everything else – the panorama of cars, clouds, low-lying buildings – began to undulate like a large tapestry. The traffic sounds faded. I closed my eyes, and meditated. I felt myself relaxing, my mind clearing. When I opened my eyes, I glanced at the clock. It was 6:59. He would arrive any second now, and I was ready.

In the rear-view mirror, I caught a glimpse of a long, black limousine. It approached stealthily like a submarine, passed me, then pulled onto the shoulder. My heart jumped, and I slowly inhaled a deep breath to regain my calm. I reached for the slim leather briefcase on the passenger seat then got out of the car.

The morning air was crisp. I marched over to the right side of the limo, and stood there. I could see his imposing silhouette in the back seat. I had met him only twice before in person. He was a massive man, not overweight, just massive – over six feet tall with a broad face, and deep blue eyes beneath a prominent brow. The driver's door clicked open and a small mustachioed man got out and padded around the car. He walked slowly, or so it seemed. It was like everything was happening in slow motion. I looked down at my watch and gazed as the second hand paused then stuttered forward, paused then stuttered forward again. An eternity later, the driver opened the back passenger door for me and ushered me inside.

I slid along the cool leather, and settled into the seat beside him. "Good morning, Rolf," I said, reaching for a handshake.

He snatched my hand, tugged at it quickly, "You have fifteen minutes."

I opened the clasps on my briefcase and removed a set of six proposals, each one a variation on a $2-million insurance policy. As far as Rolf was concerned that was why I wanted to meet with him – to discuss the $2-million proposal. In truth, I had an ulterior motive, and I needed a couple of minutes at the end of the meeting to discuss the real reason I wanted to see him. I prayed he would make up his mind about the $2 million quickly.

"Rolf," I said, "here are six proposals based on the zero-cost concept I discussed with you over the phone. The death benefit returns the original face amount, plus the premiums, plus what those premiums would have earned had you invested them elsewhere."

Rolf took the proposals from me, and studied them, spending about twenty seconds on each. The fifth proposal would be my recommendation. The premium stream and the interest rate involved best suited his needs. If he selected the fifth proposal, I would have time left to discuss the real reason for my visit. I prayed hard. While Rolf continued to look at the proposals, I placed my hands on my lap and concentrated on steadying them. I have a tendency to tap my fingers nervously, and now would be a rather untimely occasion to indulge in a distracting habit. I turned to look outside and watched as one bird chased another around in the air. Perhaps the pursuer was trying to sell the other insurance.

After two minutes, Rolf looked up. "Proposal number five," he declared.

"That is my recommendation."

"Fine, then, thank you, David."

"Rolf," I said, "I still have eleven more minutes of your time–"

Rolf looked at his watch.

"So you do," he said. I knew Rolf was a man of his word.

"Rolf, I would like to meet with you and your lawyers and

accountants. I want to develop a package of insurance for the new partnership – based on this zero-cost plan. Can we arrange an appointment to discuss this?" I asked.

Rolf was the de facto head partner of a packaging company that was undergoing a massive restructuring. I had done insurance for the original partnership years before when they bought out an international company. It was my biggest case – a total of $42 million of insurance. But since then, the company had grown tremendously. Now the insurance need would be around $100,000,000 – and I wanted a shot at the business. The fact that I had done the original insurance would help me – but not as much as I would like. Each of the 10 partners would be bringing in their own agents and the competition would be fierce. But I knew Rolf was the kingpin, whoever had his support would likely win the business. I needed him to agree to an appointment. His eyes turned and he looked me straight in the face, as though he were probing my mind for any weakness. If I flinched, he would say no. It was as simple as that.

I stared back unblinking. Rolf said yes.

Break through to selling megacases

As I drove back home, barely aware of the road and the increasing traffic, I wondered how in the world I had found myself in a position where I was asking a client for an appointment to discuss $100,000,000 worth of insurance. Thirty years earlier I had arrived in Toronto as an immigrant – virtually penniless. And somehow, since then, I had managed to rise to the top of the insurance business. As I thought about it, I realized that the answer was not really a mystery. In fact, the meeting with Rolf was an inevitable milestone on the path that I had chosen and created for myself. Since those first days in Canada, I had dreamed that I would meet people like Rolf, earn their confidence and do business with them. This book is about the strategies I developed to help me realize those dreams.

I have written this book in the hope that others might be able to use some of my strategies to realize their own dreams. The truth is, if I can do it, so can you. I have never felt I was a natural salesperson. When I was a young agent, I would marvel at the ease with which the other new salespeople seemed to sell. If they made it look easy, I made it look difficult. But, because I wasn't a natural, I was forced to develop strategies to help me sell, first small insurance policies, then larger and larger ones, until I eventually broke through to selling megacases – cases where the insurance amount is $10 million or more. In this book, I will show you all of the strategies I used to take my business and sales to the top. And, yes, I will tell you how the case with Rolf turned out – but first, the lean years.

The 8 Best Practices of High-Performing Advisors Program

Take the 8 Best Practices of High-Performing Advisors Program and increase your revenue by a minimum of 50-200% in the first two years. Over the course of this program of one-on-one coaching, self-study and workshops, you will discover how to increase your revenue year after year for the rest of your career.

You will learn how to:

- Apply the 8 Best Practices of High-Performing Salespeople
- Find and keep quality clients
- Manage a lifelong business, not just make sales

"We believe 100% in the 8 Best Practices course. It has changed the way we do business. It has shown us how to identify target markets, and develop a plan to effectively penetrate them. Now the average income of our client base is over $400,000 annually and their average net worth is over $1 million. Several of our associates and clients have also experienced the success of this course in a variety of businesses."

Robert G. Murray and R. Stewart Gavin,
Senior Vice-Presidents, Corporate Planning Associates

To enroll or to find out more about the 8 Best Practices course contact:

The Covenant Group
BCE Place, 161 Bay St.
Suite 1320, Box 529
Toronto, Ontario Canada M5J 2S1
tel: 416 304-1766 fax: 416 955-0418
email: info@covenantgroup.com

New from Norm Trainor:

The Entrepreneurial Challenge:
Building Your Business CD ROM

This CD ROM is an interactive guide to creating and implementing a business plan that works. It captures the experience of working one-on-one with Norm Trainor. He walks you through the steps involved in growing your business over the next 5 years. Using a combination of a full-length audio interview, striking visuals and interactive exercises, Norm shows you how to:

- **Create and implement your vision, mission and values**
- **Define your business opportunity**
- **Analyze your current situation**
- **Develop marketing, sales, service and resource plans**

The CD's comprehensive set of financial statements enables you to project your business performance and monitor its success.

To order or find out more about this CD contact:

The Covenant Group
BCE Place, 161 Bay St.
Suite 1320, Box 529
Toronto, Ontario
Canada M5J 2S1
tel: 416 304-1766
fax: 416 955-0418
email: info@covenantgroup.com

NORM TRAINOR
The Entrepreneurial Challenge
Building Your Business
An Interactive Guide to Creating and Implementing Your Business Plan
• Define your business
• Set attainable objectives
• Create effective strategies
• Financial management

The Covenant Group

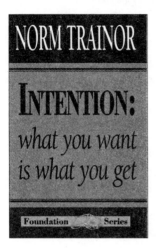

Praise for David Cowper's

Breakthrough

"Breakthrough is far and away the best book on selling life insurance that I have read. Most books deal with 'cutesy' ideas or read like textbooks; whereas this one reads more like a novel, making it fast-paced and highly readable. Our industry would be a far more credible place to work, with a much better image, if we had more professionals like David Cowper."

Walter C. Barclay, BA, CFP, CLU, CH.F.C, Walter C. Barclay Insurance Agency

"Breakthrough is a most unusual book. At first I thought I was reading a 'James Bond Spy Adventure.' This is such a pleasant change from the usual type of sales book. It is like reading a novel — you can't put it down. Great Work!"

David Baird, CLU, A.I.I.C., C.F.S.B., Ten Star Life Insurance Brokers Inc.

"David Cowper is a true visionary in our business. This book is a great read for all salespersons, but it is a must-read for those selling life insurance. We all owe you thanks for writing this book."

Paul W. Fincham, Executive Planning International Life Insurance Limited

"No matter what your industry, no matter what your product, if you want to sell in the big leagues, this book is a revelation."

Steve Carlson, Publisher and Editor, Marketing Options

"Well done! This book is a real winner. I could not put it down until I finished it. It captured my mind from the first page to the last page."

Keith Coles, CFP, CLU, CH.F.C, The Coles Group Inc.

"David Cowper is not just one of the world's most successful life insurance salespeople; he is one of the cleverest. He thinks his way into giant cases and so can we, if we follow his strategies."

Tony Gordon, Past Chairman, Top of the Table, Bristol, England

"This is a powerful book. It is motivational, inspirational as well as instructive. It has drama, humor, and pathos."

Phil Carroll, President, Fifer Financial Services Inc.

How to get HIGHRISE products

- To get copies of HIGHRISE books, check your local bookstore or on-line retailer.
- To get copies of HIGHRISE audio cassettes as well as HIGHRISE books:
    In the US, call Lexington House at 1-800-356-5936
    In Canada, call CAIFA at 1-800-307-0206
  Discounts available for bulk orders.

HiGHRise
BOOKS ™

Norm Trainor speaks at seminars, conventions and to
organizations all over the world. To book him for speaking
engagements, contact:

VORG Incorporated
Financial Speakers and Trainers Group
555 Richmond Street West
Suite 1008, P.O. Box 214
Toronto, Ontario, Canada, M5V 3B1

Tel: (416) 703-8674
Fax: (416) 703-8675
1-800-694-VORG (8674)

Norm is always pleased to hear from his readers.
You can reach him at:

The Covenant Group

BCE Place, 161 Bay St.
Suite 1320, Box 529
Toronto, Ontario
Canada M5J 2S1

tel: 416 304-1766 fax: 416 955-0418
email: info@covenantgroup.com